NORMAL PEOPLE'S THOUGHTS ON *THE 50% RULE*

"*The 50% Rule* entirely breaks the mold when it comes to how we can and should work differently and more authentically. Erin's 50% Rule approach has given me the permission to be unapologetically who I am and work in a way that is aligned with my personal values and mission."

–Heather Pierce, a working mother who isn't a *New York Times* bestselling author but does have a *New York Times* subscription

"It's impossible to think of this as a rule when it's so much fun. If you hate reinventing the wheel but thrive on improving it, do yourself a favor—get this book! *The 50% Rule* will give you your time, sanity, and life back! This is not just a book or a principle—it's a lifestyle!"

–Mari Dertinger, pump-wearing, brush-wielding, avant-garde artist pushing the envelope to make her mark in corporate America

"It was hard to focus on just two sentences to write; there's so much gold in this book. *The 50% Rule* has been a life-changing, viewpoint-altering, new dynamic that I have infused into my whole life. This book will trigger your inner creative and help you add YOU to everything you do!"

–Bill McCormick, founder of Digi-Sales, author of *The Social Sales Compass*, and just a normal everyday entrepreneur

"If you are starting your career, transforming it, or guiding a team that would benefit from a zhuzh, this book will give you a ridiculously simple but industrial-strength framework to help you put on your big-kid pants and brave the path less traveled. I noted and dog-eared just about every page."

–Michelle L. Gardner, a non-PhD university leader who connects those who want to change the world with those who can, aka Professional Enabler

"Most of my reading is nonfiction, self-help-y, business books. And I have some simple rules: the book must provide at least one thing of value, and the writing can't make me want to poke my eyes out because it's preachy and snoozy. *The 50% Rule* takes its own advice, giving you a book that is only about half like a normal one and half like a page-turning crime thriller (without the bloodshed . . . unless you count the papercuts as I dog-eared pages). Ready to transform your career, work, and life? You gotta read this book!"

–HP, not Harry Potter or Hewlett Packard, just a guy who actually read the book (twice) before throwing out a review

PRAISE FOR ERIN'S FIRST BOOK, *YOU DO YOU(ISH)*

★★★★★ Raw, relevant, fricking hilarious, and a game changer

"I'm really not one to pick up self-help-type books . . . but this one hooked me on page one. I was standing reading this in my kitchen, laying in my seven-year-old's bed, wherever I could keep reading it. I laughed so much. Erin is raw and hilarious, and it felt like talking to a friend over wine about your career woes. I self-reflected often and had inner dialogue with myself, having so many realizations as I read every page. And there are so many memorable and practical tools to take away from this that I can and already have immediately applied in my life. This book is a game-changer."

★★★★★ *Motivational, inspirational, helpful and hilarious!*

"Normally it takes me weeks (sometimes months) to get through a book, especially a nonfiction one, and then *You Do You(ish)* came along, and I read it in less than a week, a new record for me. I almost felt like this book was written for me. This book provides motivation and inspiration without an in-your-face approach, but one that makes so much sense and feels like your best friend giving you advice and *a-ha* moments. I love it and I think anyone looking for the strategies to keep moving forward in his/her career should read this immediately!"

★★★★★ **Expect to enjoy this "self-help" book!**

"This book is captivating, even if you are in a negative place where everything just seems like it's 'game over' and you're going to have to settle (don't do it!). Erin's voice will grow inside your head—she is electrifying . . . fun and witty. The Six Principles of Strategic Authenticity are core points throughout the book—Erin does a great job making meaningful connections that are personal so you can actually apply them through your journey. This book helped me navigate a very challenging time in my life. It's because of Erin's voice and guidance through this book, I can honestly share that I am in a much better place today."

THE 50% RULE

Throw Out Half the Playbook
to Start Competing in a League of Your Own

THE 50% RULE

ERIN HATZIKOSTAS

Urano
publishing
Argentina - Chile - Colombia - Spain
USA - Mexico - Peru - Uruguay

The first edition of this book was published in October 2024.

ISBN: 978-19-53027-44-3

E-ISBN: 978-1-953027-45-0

Printed in Colombia

Library of Cataloging-in-Publication Data

Hatzikostas, Erin

1. Personal Growth   2. Business

To all the underdogs out there who are exhausted from working so damn hard to get ahead.

Table of Contents

Preface

About halfway through writing this book, something half-magical, half-creepy happened: I started referring to it as my BFF.

I couldn't stop thinking about the book. I wanted to be with it and in it whenever I could. I carried the book everywhere I went. I'd throw my computer in the car when I ran to get my kids from practice, just in case I had ten minutes to spare while waiting. I went from dread to delight when I realized my son had a longer hockey practice; I couldn't wait to use that forced alone time to work on the book. I even sent an email to my literary agent (whom I'd only known for a few weeks) that said, "Still writing like a mad woman. Super-duper weird, but this book has become my BFF. It's not a book; it's a vibe."

If you're like me, you're equal parts high achiever, equal parts head case. When you put your mind to something, watch out, nothing'll stop ya. But other times, you're like, "WTF? Why can't I even take one step forward?!"

I'm not a disciplined person. I struggle with lists and project plans. I would never describe myself as "gritty." Yet I've somehow accomplished big things in my life. I was the CEO of a company with 1,000 employees. I started my own business. I gave a TEDx Talk, and this is my second book. But if I'm not disciplined, then how in the heck did I do all those things?

The 50% Rule.

Over the next 250ish pages, we'll get into what this wild and mysterious rule is, but I first want to say I hope it helps you experience what I experienced while working on this book. Writing my first book was a love/hate process. At times, I loved pounding the keyboard with my thoughts. But most of the time, I had to set goals, I dreaded rewrites, and admittedly, when I got to the two-yard line, I closed my eyes, punted the ball to my editor, and hoped for the best.

But my experience this time was completely different. I could not wait to have time to work on the book. Sometimes to write a chapter. Sometimes to do light editing. Sometimes to get deep into research. Sometimes to just sit in my thoughts on how to make it better.

This was NOT me before writing this book. It almost felt like the cosmic impact of The Rule on both a micro and macro level.

More than anything, this is what I want for you. Once you've read the book and practiced The Rule, I hope you fully feel its power. I hope you'll be excited to do big things. I hope you'll trade a nap on a Sunday for a chance to work on your passion. I predict that things you accomplished before, only by deploying torturous productivity hacks, will now get done with limited effort. I'm confident you will go from *having* to do stuff to *wanting* to do stuff.

I want you to be successful. Get that promotion, explode your business, create the next viral TikTok—whatever it is that goes waaaaay beyond your wildest dreams. However, what I want most is for you to walk through work and life feeling like your big, hairy, audacious goals are no longer a burden; they're your new BFFs.

Until then, I hope *The 50% Rule* becomes your new BFF.

Introduction

What does it take to turn a simple idea into a worldwide sensation, without the discipline, misery, and sacrifice that most big things *seem* to require? Sam Balto, a physical education teacher from Oregon, did just that when he 50% Ruled transportation at his elementary school. But that's a story for later.

The 50% Rule is simple on the surface but intricate and powerful at its core. That is, any time you're doing something new, taking advice, or trying to get ahead, always look to do 50 percent the normal way and the other 50 percent a new way. If we were to visualize it, it would look something like this:

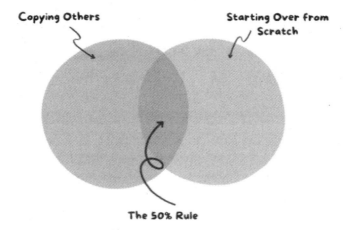

Copying Others

Starting Over from Scratch

The 50% Rule

However, I can't let you drop in and plummet five feet down to The Rule. You need to hear stories first to understand The Rule's gears, components, and features. You need an on-ramp to Balto's story to ensure you understand that The 50% Rule is more than just a gnarly mantra; it's the secret weapon behind extraordinary successes. And it should be something you can't stop thinking about, using, and loving.

Beyond Balto, you'll uncover what happened when a singer decided to alter a sacred tradition. You'll follow the journey of a top-notch nerd who went from being bullied to acclaimed. You'll be inspired by two people who almost didn't pursue their dream careers but then used The Rule to help them say "yes."

You'll read catchy quotes, and I'll offer up ridiculous metaphors. If you're human, you'll laugh and get verklempt. You'll spend time with Lin-Manuel Miranda, Ruth Bader Ginsburg, and the Savannah Bananas. You'll hear stories of other well-known people, as well as everyday warriors like you. These stories are woven together because they used The 50% Rule to throw out half the playbook so they could start competing in a league of their own. And, of course, you'll hear my stories too: your 50% Rule crash test dummy.

I'm excited to spend the next few hours, days, or weeks with you. Know that I'm not the writer of this book. I'm the host of your 50% Rule road trip. Enjoy the vibe and the ride!

SECTION 1:

· · · · · · · · · · · · · · ·

STOP 100%ING

1
Joyception Day

Did you take Calculus in school? If you did, there's a good chance you remember the specific day you got hit over the head with something that felt like both joy and deception—joyception.

For months, you painstakingly learned a gazillion complicated ways to determine the derivative of an equation. Your teacher taught you all this fancy stuff about how the derivative is the rate of change of a function and that it's also the tangent line to the curve. You whipped out your graphing calculator. You sweated it out. You did math gymnastics you never thought possible. You followed every formula your teacher kept throwing your way.

But then the day of joyception arrived. Your teacher stood in front of your class and said something like, *Hey, no biggie, but yeah, there's also a shortcut to all this rocket science I've been teaching you. You can just take the exponent, place it in front of the equation, and then subtract one from the exponent and place it back up there.*

What the f*********** . . . yay?!

That's what I was thinking, and I'm guessing it was your reaction too. Joy and deception at the same time. Joyception to the nth degree.

You know what, here's the hard truth: We *had* to learn all those other formulas and challenging stuff. It gave us context. It was calisthenics for our brain. It gave us options. It made us smarter and stronger.

And it's the same for The 50% Rule. For years, I've been obsessed with helping people and companies use authenticity as their secret weapon, their strategic advantage. It's what my entire first book, *You Do You(ish): Unleash Your Authentic Superpowers to Get the Career You Deserve*, was about. I've been providing a formula/prescription/training wheels to help people change their mindsets and actions in the workplace for years.

But I realized I had a shortcut—actually, a Swiss Army Knife—to using authenticity in my back pocket all along. It was The 50% Rule. It can help you do authenticity every day. It's also a tool that will make imposter syndrome impossible, comparisons irrelevant, move you from poser to pioneer, and—my favorite—make everything you do exponentially more fun. Yes, pun intended.

I was excited to write this book. The 50% Rule had germinated in my head, then spread to my coaching and consulting. It had become a mantra I could not stop using and reciting.

Thoughts of this silly rule becoming the basis of my second book insisted on percolating. For nine months, I kept a digital note on my phone with every story, observation, and thought I had about The 50% Rule. I was obsessed. I was ready. It was going to be EPIC!

Until . . . my excitement came to a screeching halt.

I had to write a book proposal.

You see, I wanted this book to be traditionally published, which means that instead of going off like a bat outta hell and putting together a book on my own, like I did for my first book, I wanted to partner with a formal publisher to birth this baby.

Here's a little inside baseball: To traditionally publish a book, you have to write a book proposal. And book proposals have a formula.

You might say, *A formula?! Yay! There's a tried and true blueprint you just need to learn, work hard at, do well, and then, you're rollin'? That sounds fantastic.* Well, for me, a formula kinda feels like when I volunteer to be a chaperone for my kid's field trip. It seems like a fun thing to do until I'm on the bus with seventy snot-nosed, screaming kids, and then I want to jump out the window. Immediately.

Writing my first book taught me this about myself: When I'm *supposed* to do something, I lose my shit. And in that book, I beat it into your head:

You shouldn't not do something because you hate the way it's been done before. Instead, do it your own way.

I know I'm not alone in this. Following someone else's formula sounds fantastic until you're on a bus to hell and don't know how you got there.

In *You Do You(ish)*, I shared my insight into how authenticity was the key to my career and business success. And I gave a—oh God, here it goes—*formula* for you to leverage so you could use authenticity as your secret weapon to success. Now, before you call me a hypocrite, nothing I preach in that book, including my Six Principles of Strategic Authenticity framework (H.U.M.A.N.S.), is a fraud. It's just that there's another layer—maybe even some cheat code—that makes it easier to use authenticity to your advantage.

I can't wait to share more about this cheat code so we can propel YOU into a league of *your* own.

2
Sleeprunning Syndrome

Somewhere between miles two and three, I thought, *What in the hell is going on?!*

I'm a runner. Not a super amazing, highly competitive runner, but I enjoy running. I mostly do it to be social, get fresh air, and feel less guilty when I want to eat chocolate after every meal.

Although I've run several races over the years, I'm not a big fan of doing them. Nearly every race I've done was because my friends had the idea, and I didn't want to be the lame-o who said "no."

It was always a bit odd to me, though: My friends get all jacked up to run races, while instead I secretly scour my brain for the best excuse to opt out. It's weird because I played sports growing up and consider myself a sports-watching junkie. I love to compete. I love to be around people. And I love to run. So why don't I love to do running sports competitions?

This particular day, I was running my fourth half-marathon. Yes, the only marathons I've run are 50% marathons. Predictable, I know.

Anyway, I was in relatively good shape—better than I'd been for other races. Not only had I stuck to a training routine, but I had also been doing yoga regularly, which made me feel stronger than I'd ever felt. But not long into the race, I noticed something. More people were passing me than usual.

One of the unavoidable mindfucks of running a longer race is you can't help but keep track of if you're passing people or if, instead, it seems like everyone is passing you. It's a natural barometer of whether or not you're having a good race. During this race, I noticed that I was getting passed by more people than I passed myself, and the ratio felt more uneven than in any of my previous races.

I assessed: *Did I start too far towards the front of the pack?* Nope. *Did I feel slower or weaker than I had felt in other races?* Nope. *Then why am I getting passed by so many people?!*

I couldn't help it. I knew I wouldn't win or even place in the Top 10. But I still couldn't stop continuously comparing myself to other runners for 13.1 miles.

Oddly, despite how I was perceiving my performance, I finished the race with my second-best 50% marathon time. As I crossed the finish line, though, I still felt poopy. Others beat me. Others passed me. Others had better times.

After limping through the chute and grabbing my medal and bottle of water, I walked back up the course on the sideline. My friends were behind me, and I wanted to cheer them on as they finished the race. As I waited for them and rooted on the other runners, a moment of "Huh?" slowly built until it crescendoed into a full-fledged "OH?!" There were a shit-ton of people behind me.

Here's the thing: it's easy to get a Comparison Cramp when you're running a race—a rigid, pre-defined, sanctioned race. A race where everyone runs the same route, heading for the same exact finish line. Looking ahead of you and seeing the people who are beating you is easy. And it sucks. Looking behind you and seeing people trailing you is much more difficult.

I thought, *What an incredible metaphor. You must be sure to also look BEHIND you when comparing yourself to others.* Amazing, right?

Actually, no, it's not. I realized: THAT'S NOT THE RIGHT MESSAGE!

Instead, you need to get rid of the race altogether! Ditch the predefined path with the traffic cones and the water stations, the precise starting times and the rankings of first to worst. Scrap the idea that we're all meant to travel down the same path and not allowed to veer off and run down a side road or create our own path altogether. That's the real lesson here. And that's the lesson of this book.

Stop racing and start embracing 50%.

You might not want to hear this, but even if you're like, [insert snarky, nasally voice for drama] *Well, I'm not even a runner*, you likely have Sleeprunning Syndrome (SS).

No, you don't have Sleep*walking* Syndrome. You run. You're running every day. You're running to complete a big project on time. You're running to clear as many emails as possible. You're running to build your business faster and better than everyone else. You're running to pick up your daughter from soccer practice.

You're running to please your boss. You're running to get the daily gold medal of likeability, fortune, and success. Like a treadmill that won't shut off, you're running. You're running. You're running.

You know this. But sadly, what you haven't had time to think about is that you're also sleeping. Yes, you have great ideas. Yes, you put thought into that PowerPoint you're crafting. Yes, you think hard about what to make for dinner while driving to get your daughter.

However, there's a problem in there . . . In all your running, you often don't have time to slow down and think, question things, or think about alternative options. You want to be a rebel. You try to bring your authenticity to everything you do. You know you prefer to be bold and different. But, ironically, your running is largely prohibiting all that. And all your Sleeprunning is manifesting itself into some crappy symptoms.

If you're still thinking, with your same snarky 'tude, *Yes, I am running, but I'm awake. I'm aware. I'm not Sleeprunning.* If that's the case, then it's important to better understand the symptoms of the disease. Here are the most common symptoms of Sleeprunning Syndrome (SS):

- Comparison Cramps: You often find yourself comparing, competing, and/or chasing others.

- Copying Calluses: You're impressed by what worked for others and get frustrated when you can't do it as well.

- Perfection Pain: You fear getting things "wrong" more than you desire doing things differently.

- Self-Doubt Gout: You have lots of great ideas but often stop yourself in your tracks in case they're silly or stupid.

- Finish Fatigue: You love doing new things, but you have a million unfinished new things.

- Pioneer Paralysis: Being bold and innovative sounds amazing but is ultimately daunting and paralyzing.

* If you have two or more of these symptoms, keep reading this book.

While symptoms vary from person to person, there's a common path—a typical order of operations—that will turn what feels like a common cold into an uncontrollable fever.

The first thing that usually pops up is **Comparison Cramps**. You notice what someone else is doing and think that they're doing it better, with more ease, or with an authority you don't think you have. You compare yourself to peers at work, people on Instagram, and your friends. You compare your business to others'. You compare how your meeting went versus another meeting you attended later that day. You compare yourself to your best friends and complete strangers. And you NEVER adjust your comparisons. You compare your three-month struggle to people's ten-year journey. You compare your stock price to that of a company that is twenty times bigger. You compare the cleanliness of your house to your stay-at-home friend's house. Every day, you're comparing.

Then, you think you know the cure to your annoying little Comparison Cramps: copy others. If you just start copying what others are doing, those cramps will magically disappear. Because that's what you're taught to do, right? Since you were a baby and watched your parents walk and talk, you've been copying. You've been taught that to succeed, you should emulate those around you. But because you're running so damn fast—copying, copying—the next thing you know, you have

Copying Calluses everywhere. They hurt. They slow you down. They make you miserable.

And you think, *I know how to get rid of these. I just need a bit more discipline, and I will become as awesome as [X person] is!* You read productivity books, write (and rewrite) your to-do list, block your calendar. You get atomic, deploy seven highly effective habits, and eat some frogs. You might even go all ninja and start using the work-in-timed-intervals Pomodoro Technique. Because that must be the difference between you and them. They have discipline. You don't. But gosh darn it, you WILL transform yourself into the Taskinator. You think, *Let's goooooo!*

Then, one morning, you go to bed all Pomodorable and wake up Pomodone. Instead of being ready for another day of taskinating, you can't even get one foot out of bed. You're exhausted and ache all over. You gather just enough strength to telemed with your doctor, who promptly tells you it must be **Perfection Pain,** a common symptom of Sleeprunning Syndrome. She tells you that when you work that hard, focusing on comparing and copying, it's common to come down with Perfection Pain. She prescribes you a pill and explains that it should help wipe away your pain.

You take the pill and decide to take the day off to rest in bed. You're happy the doctor seems to have a cure for your pain. But, as you lie there, you feel a new symptom come on: **Self-Doubt Gout.** You think, *Why are others better than me at enduring the pain it takes to do big shit? They probably don't need a pill; they probably push through it.* You start to convince yourself that you're just wired differently. Duh. You're not as smart, as disciplined, or as gifted as they are. You start to laugh at yourself and wonder, *How did I ever think that* I *could actually do what they do? I'm just not meant for things THAT big.*

You reflect on all that dreaming and work and discipline you've been doing. And in an instant, you feel like a Pomodork. That energy and excitement you once had to go for the big job, start your own company, host a great party, invent a new product, lead something big at your company was just that: a dream. A few moments later, you feel a huge wave of something half-exhausting, half-relieving pass over you: **Finish Fatigue.**

You quickly notice it. You've felt this before. But this time, you don't fight it. You recognize that your Finish Fatigue is just too much to overcome. Maybe you could bust through it if you were still twenty-three. If you didn't work sixty hours a week. If you didn't have two little ones. If you weren't married. If you didn't have a mortgage and car payments and a never-ending adulting list. But nope, you're running too hard. Your cramps, calluses, pain, and gout make it impossible to conceive how you could possibly fight through Finish Fatigue.

Finally, as you lie in bed, a pint of chocolate ice cream in one hand and a TV remote in the other, your dreams of being a pioneer in this world . . . die. **Pioneer Paralysis** shows up like Glinda the Good Witch in *The Wizard of Oz*. She gently takes the spoon out of your hand and does a little tap-tap on your forehead. Not hard. Light. Like Glinda did for Dorothy, Pioneer Paralysis calms you down and then gives you the sweet little permission you need to return to your warm, cozy comfort zone. *Your* version of Kansas. The place that feels just right for someone who's just not meant to be big city folk. Someone who is *supposed* to be in "Kansas." Someone who is okay with just good enough. Because you've seen what it takes to be great. And man-oh-man, you are just not cut out for that. There's just too much running and pain and disease outside of "home."

This is the cycle of Sleeprunning Syndrome. It gives you just enough pain to warn you, but not enough to kill you. Just enough pain to make things hard. But not so much that you don't ever come back to the cycle. While it sucks, the worst thing about the syndrome is that it's often not acute enough for you to want to get a vaccine or go to physical therapy to prevent it from returning. And, look, you shouldn't be embarrassed about your SS. I'm here to expose it and also normalize it. I have it too! SS is like chicken pox; it's dormant in nearly all of us. My unscientific epidemiology on SS is that it's grown increasingly prevalent due to:

- Warp-speed working conditions: The speed at which business and life have continuously grown has us all running faster than we ever imagined.

- Technology: The ability to learn from others, whether it's via social media, online courses, blogs, etc., has exploded. So has our exposure to more people to compare ourselves to.

- Goodwill: Yes, more and more people are (well-meaningly!) looking to dole out their formulas and wisdom to others, but that can have unintentional negative consequences that lead to SS.

• • • • • • • • • • • • •

We spend too much time either copying others' formulas or trying to build a completely new spaceship. In the middle of these two approaches lies a beautiful place of growth, innovation, and leadership that feels way less icky and also brings new, better stuff into the world.

• • • • • • • • • • • •

It's time for you to get comfortable in the middle ground between going rogue and starting from scratch . . . to realize you don't have to live in "Kansas," but also don't have to move to "New York City." In fact, I'm here to teach you that by not choosing EITHER of those "homes," but instead creating your own new home with everything you do, you will severely minimize your Sleeprunning Syndrome symptoms. This book is your SS vaccine. The more you use The 50% Rule, the more you'll send SS into remission. It will rear its head less and less. The 50% Rule will help you click your red sneakers together to break free of Sleeprunning Syndrome. Cure the cramps. Fix the fatigue. Propel the pioneer in you.

Do half. Become whole.

3

Glass Half-Empty

My friend Scott Mason, a transformational coach and podcast host, asked if I could hop on a call so he could get my advice on something. When I answered, he almost immediately professed, "Thank you again for introducing me to Brand Builders Group, but I think I'm going to quit." He explained that the program was amazing, but it was too formulaic for him. Because he's a creative, free spirit, it just wasn't a good fit.

Brand Builders Group (BBG) is a program I joined in 2019 to help me build my business. I had just retired as the CEO of an approximately 1,000-person financial healthcare company and made my first crack at being an entrepreneur. I knew I had a lot to learn, so I joined BBG to show me "the way."

So, when Scott came to me about three months after joining BBG and told me it wasn't working for him, I was shocked. And then, three seconds later, I wasn't shocked. It hit me that he was probably right where I was about three months into joining the group as well: overwhelmed and feeling like what they were teaching me was probably effective but not exactly "me."

For most of my life, I've been a high achiever. Not all the time, but on a broad level, I've been successful. At the same time, I can also be a head case; my biggest flaw is that I don't consider myself disciplined. Following any sort of project plan, or even a numbered list in order, gives me the heebie-jeebies. I literally cannot do it. At the same time, I work my ass off. I'm not lazy. In the first three years running my own business, I published my first book, did a TEDx Talk, led a primary research project, spoke/led workshops for forty-plus organizations, hosted a podcast that now has over 200 episodes, and cranked out hundreds of blogs, articles, quizzes, guides, etc.

But like Scott, I also hit a massive wall with Brand Builders Group. In my logical brain, everything they were teaching me as the formula for success made sense. At the same time, executing it all made me feel icky, stressed, and unmotivated.

And then one day, I was sitting in a session—stirring in my seat and my thoughts—and I randomly thought: *What if I 50% Ruled what they're teaching me?*

Until then, The 50% Rule was something I had been using under a different context. I had spewed out this rule years earlier while giving career advice. The OG 50% Rule was something I would say to encourage someone to insist that their next job make them feel 50 percent uncomfortable. It was my way of making it more tangible that if you want to grow in your career, each next step has to happen outside your comfort zone. It wasn't a rule I formed from something I read or heard from someone else; it came organically when I diagnosed what I had accidentally done each step in my career, and how much that ~50 percent uncomfortableness had propelled me forward.

So, as I sat in that Brand Builders Group session, I metaphorically dug into the box in my closet that houses all the seasonal home decor I barely use but save just in case. I realized that a less-in-use picture frame might have a new, more powerful use. The 50% Rule had always helped me grow as I climbed the traditional corporate ladder, but now I needed an even more robust frame(work).

I thought, *The 50% Rule could also mean I should only take about 50 percent of what I'm learning from the Brand Builders Group. The other 50 percent I should do my own way.* And that's The 50% Rule: Merge half-normal with half-new.

The 50% Rule: Merge half-normal with half-new.

Yes, the *foundation* of The Rule is that simple. Each time you learn something new, are stuck at a wall, are looking to create something new, etc., only take about half of what others teach you or already do as "normal" and then blend that with about half of something different, better, or that is simply more *you*.

The 50% Rule came to me spontaneously in the moment, but I quickly realized why The Rule is so powerful.

We often think of things as binary options. On one side of the binary bus, you hear things like, "Just do it your way" or "You do you, boo!" While that sounds exciting and empowering at first, as you start to metaphorically wear your underwear on the *outside* of your pants, you quickly feel awkward . . . nervous that "your way" feels more like you, but also leaves you exposed and vulnerable. And so you retreat. Underwear back on the inside.

On the flip side of the binary bus of badassery rebellion is the safety of following the leader . . . playing it safe by learning from others, executing on the playbooks of the past, and doing things "right." While it may not be as fun, it feels safe and cozy. Others have proven that underwear on the inside is a better option. Why would you want to reinvent undergarments? Best to stay on the road that others have paved.

The 50% Rule gives you permission to land in the middle. Permission to, for example, wear LED-lit underwear on the inside of your pants. That is, you can do things your way AND learn from others.

The minute I hatched The 50% Rule, something magical happened. I could immediately feel the Anxiety Ants in my stomach march away and be replaced with Motivated Moths. Bum, bum, bum turned to flittery flitter. My Perfection Pain flitted away like a falcon. I felt free. I felt enabled. I felt like I could conquer the world. Instead of doing less, I was now set up to be and do more. Not more *work*. More, period. The 50% Rule creates an entirely new equation where half and half is greater than the sum of its parts. **50% + 50% > 100%.**

So, when Scott reluctantly confessed that he wanted to quit Brand Builders, I immediately and unconsciously spewed out, "What if you 50% Ruled things instead?"

I told him that I knew how he felt. I understood that much of what he was learning was rigid and formulaic and, quite frankly, took a lot of work. But I also told him that he, like me, also needs some corralling. Even though we're free spirits, we also need some rules. We need ideas on how to frame our thoughts. We need processes . . . at least a few.

I went on to give him an example of what I learned in their sessions on writing a book. I explained that I decided to scrap some things they taught—things I *should* do to promote my book, but things that felt exhausting and inauthentic, like hosting webinars or renting a tour bus. At the same time, I told him what I learned about structure and pithy statements. I told him I credit these things for the success of my first book. If I had written that book without guidance from BBG, the book would have been entertaining and insightful, but not actionable.

And to be clear: The 50% Rule isn't about doing things half-assed; it's about ditching about half of what you learn or is status quo so you can make room to add in other ideas that help you fill in the puzzle differently. For example, I knew that while *You Do You(ish)* was primarily guided by my experiences and stories, I did not want to write a memoir.

But instead of flipping the memoir switch to "off," I decided to half-ish do a memoir by simply adding short bursts of personal anecdotes to my book. By giving myself permission to 50% Rule it, I escaped the binary decision of memoir/no-memoir and simply did it my own way.

I wanted the same for Scott. While quitting isn't always a bad thing, I knew how much he would benefit from sticking with the program, but only if he applied The 50% Rule.

It was the first time I shared my rule with someone else, so my conviction quickly was replaced by me, elbows on my desk, leaning in with intense curiosity: "Does this make sense to you?"

Scott replied immediately, "Oh my God, you're right. I don't necessarily have to take or do everything I learn. Even if I take

50 percent of it, and then the other 50 percent in a way that feels more like me, I'll be in a much better place."

You don't have to *comply* with the rules. Instead, learn the rules and then *create* your own jewels.

Not only is The 50% Rule a selfish mantra to help you move forward, but it's also what people on the "other side" are craaaaving too. Customers, colleagues, friends, students, employees—they NEED you to 50% Rule things so they can also see fresh, innovative, new, and authentic things.

I know you're likely thinking, *OK, got it. This is great. And you know what? This just put a name to what I strive to do every day. But I certainly don't need to read another 200+ pages to keep getting it and getting it and getting it.*

And hey, no judgment if you stop right here. But I promise you this: I do not do ANYTHING as an exercise in futility. Futility is my kryptonite. So, know that I would not have written another 200+ pages if I didn't believe with all my soul that you need more.

Not only am I certain that if you don't read on, you'll have massive holes in your 50% Rule modus operandi (I continue to have holes, AND I'M WRITING A DAMN BOOK ABOUT IT!), but you'll also miss out on its full power.

My goal is that you finish this book journey with much more than a mantra. You exit with a full-on 50% Rule makeover.

• • • • • • • • • • • •

Stop copying. Start curating.

• • • • • • • • • • • •

4

Glass Half-Full

"Slap Ya Mama!" he yelled from the living room. "Erin, you gotta put some Slap Ya Mama on it!"

Several years ago, my father discovered Walker & Sons' Cajun Seasoning: Slap Ya Mama, and he puts it on everything. Eggs? Slap Ya Mama. Steak? Slap Ya Mama. Lasagna? Slap Ya Mama.

The 50% Rule quickly became *my* Slap Ya Mama—I started putting it on everything.

Monday, I was listening to a podcast, and I thought to myself: *Don't forget to apply The 50% Rule.*

On Tuesday, I was looking at some Pinterest pictures, seeking inspiration for a room in our house. I thought: Gonna 50% Rule this.

On Wednesday, I was coaching a client. We were updating his resume, and I sent him an example of a resume I helped another client with. He was struggling with "imitating" some of the details. I told him: "50% Rule it."

On Thursday, I asked ChatGPT to give me some podcast episode name ideas. I 50% Ruled one of their suggestions.

On Friday, I was on a call with our financial advisors. At the top of the call, the head honcho guy says, "I read your LinkedIn post about The 50% Rule. That was powerful. I'm going to use that. You should write a book about it." (Great idea.😌)

The frequency with which I used this silly little rule bordered on ridiculous. However, despite using The Rule to karate kick through so many personal barriers, my 50% Rule glass was still half-empty. The Rule was a nice half-pint of beer, but it certainly wasn't a twenty-ounce Triple IPA primed to compete at the Great American Beer Festival . . . or be the topic of an entire book.

But, as I explored and used The 50% Rule more and more, something extraordinary happened. I started to observe the world through 50% Rule glasses (no, not beer goggles). And through those lenses, it became clear that The Rule is much more than just a compromise code or a cute little reminder to "add *you* to everything you do."

I started to see that The 50% Rule was the thread, and best-kept secret, that connected some of the most successful people, products, and companies in the world.

I began to notice instances where others used The 50% Rule that resulted in everything from personal relief to groundbreaking innovation. What others might see as extraordinary talent, unreachable success, or even plain ole luck, I saw differently. I saw a pattern. I put a name to it. I noticed that people who used the principles behind The 50% Rule had massive success. They were innovating. They were altering crusty old traditions. They were creating superfans. Most importantly, they were doing these big things without pain and suffering; instead, they were doing them with fun and ease.

It was like when you finally decide on the new car you want to buy, and then in some karmic craziness, you start to see that car every-frickin'-where. I saw The 50% Rule in *America's Got Talent*, *Hamilton*, the Savannah Bananas, *South Park*, *The Office*, and many other places.

I used it in numerous coaching calls and conversations with friends.

I started prefacing every piece of advice I gave with The Rule.

And I built additional "infrastructure" and frameworks to put it into practice at a grander scale.

I'm excited to give you the most versatile seasoning you've ever carried around. This seasoning will help you go from chasing, comparing, and changing for others to becoming a pioneer, thought leader, and doing just about everything authentically your own way. My favorite thing about this rule and the journey you're about to embark on is that The 50% Rule will also make everything you do SO much more fun. It certainly has for me.

Well, except for cooking. I still hate cooking, even if I have Slap Ya Mama.

So, how does this all play out from here? First, we'll etch The 50% Rule in your brain like a cute little tattoo (minus the pain and regret). We'll focus on how The Rule can help your professional growth and be your go-to Swiss Army Knife for much of what ails you today.

You'll hear stories of how the components of The Rule helped alter old traditions and create incredible connections. You'll hear the story about how a super-nerd used The 50% Rule to become a superstar. You'll assess yourself, and also probably pee yourself, when I tell you the most embarrassing story of my life. And I'll give you the inside-out scoop on how you can avoid similar perils. You'll also get some cool data and tough love thrown your way.

Then, we'll talk about your role as a mentor and advisor and how you must start walking around like a 50% Rule human billboard, making sure others don't eff themselves up taking 100 percent of your well-intentioned advice.

We'll then step up our game further in my favorite section, 50% Your Business Growth. We'll talk about how you can do more than cure your ailments—you can become a bona fide pioneer and innovator. You'll hear several stories of others who didn't just have success with The Rule, but changed the game with The Rule, and how you can do the same.

We'll then take the cute little rule and put some big-kid pants on it. I'll show you how you can do more than chant this mantra. I'll show you how you can use its souped-up version, The 50% Rule (I)nnovation Process, to lead your projects and teams in a way that's tangible and different from how you're probably Sleeprunning through innovation today. I'll give you a playbook to use on projects, with your team, and across your company.

We'll move on to talk about the profound impact The Rule can have on your *personal* life. As I met with dozens of people throughout the writing process, the transformations in their careers and work were amazing, but the transformations in their non-work lives were extraordinary.

Then, we'll uncover a surprising and supercool connection between two of the 50% Rulers from earlier in the book. Even I, the author of this book, was shocked and inspired by what I uncovered. I share how their "wedlock" can inspire and propel you even more. We'll also hit on some of the mutations this Rule can take; The 50% Rule would be a fraud if it didn't produce offspring and new uses. That's exactly what it's designed to do. And I will encourage you to morph, mod, and shape it too.

Finally, we'll bring the book together at the end in a few ways. First, I'll avail myself of The 50% Rule (JIGSAW) Puzzle Principles, a framework that binds together the top six principles demonstrated throughout the book. This will make it easier for you to continue to use The Rule to reach its ultimate power. Lastly, we will finally take a ride through the story of Sam Balto's Bike Bus and the unexpected and profound lessons this one story holds.

But most of all, along the way, you'll hear loads of stories and transformational quotes, along with some candid coaching from yours truly. My hope is that you came for the info but you stay for the vibe.

SECTION 2:

. . . .

50% YOUR PROFESSIONAL GROWTH

5

A Maddening Truth

John Madden announced his retirement at the age of forty-two. While he should have been stepping out of chaos and into calmer waters, he quickly became bored and realized he was talking to his dog way too much.

After nine years working as a head coach in the National Football League (NFL), Madden considered himself just that—a coach and nothing more. It was his identity, his passion, his love, his superpower. Like many before him, a career in football broadcasting was the obvious next step after retirement. But he didn't want to have anything to do with broadcasting.

Over the years, Madden had observed and met most of the top broadcasters. Legends like Al Michaels, Dick Enberg, and Pat Summerall had become masters of the broadcasting craft. They had put together the formula for success in NFL broadcasting. And he HATED it.

He didn't hate *them*, but he hated how broadcasting was done. He called broadcasters "Hair Dudes" and once even said that Howard Cosell was bologna. To him, broadcasting felt like a show. He thought it should be more like a classroom.

So, when CBS approached Madden to work with them as a broadcaster, he quickly said, "No, thank you." He was a coach, not a TV show. He couldn't imagine selling out and becoming just another "Hair Dude."

But regret soon sunk in. Madden realized: If he didn't take the job now, he might never get another shot at it. Like he had taught his players, you have to strike while you're a hot ticket, otherwise your ticket may expire. So, he reluctantly went back and said yes to CBS. He would test the waters as a broadcaster.

However, when he jumped on camera for the first time, rather than succumbing to Hair Dude-ness, something else happened. He 50% Ruled broadcasting.

Yes, he did turn in his signature pin-striped, short-sleeved shirt and sideline pass for a suit and tie. He cozied up with Bob Costas, a rising broadcasting star, and quickly learned the basics of broadcasting from him. But, in a twist of irony, the big-time football coach, who had literally relied on playbooks for the last decade, threw about half the broadcasting playbook out the window.

Madden brought his coaching and teaching into the booth. He whipped out a marker and drew lines and arrows over the screen to explain plays to viewers. Rather than contorting his natural voice to sound polished and rehearsed, he spoke with the same love and passion that led his former team, the Oakland Raiders, to eight playoff appearances and one Super Bowl win.

In what felt like a flash, John Madden went from hating broadcasting to loving it. Not only did he love it, but he also went on to become arguably the biggest legend in NFL broad-casting history (how else would someone get a top-selling video game named after him?)!

People quickly took notice of the authentic approach he took with the craft. Sportswriter Sam King said of Madden, "When you don't have to pretend. When you don't have to think, 'Okay, what am I going to have to say here?'—he didn't have to do that because he was always going to talk like he was talking to a guy right in front of him."

When I watched the documentary *All Madden* and learned that John Madden almost didn't go into broadcasting, I sat there dumbfounded. It hit me like the smell of fish left on a counter a day too long. I thought, *How did someone who was larger than life and made broadcasting what it was today almost not do it?!*

And then it hit me: Because no one told him he could "50% Rule it."

Certainly, no one from CBS was going to tell a newbie em-ployee to only do about half of what others were doing. Broad-casters before him, like Pat Summerall, were definitely not going to say to him, *Hey, I'm going to show you the ropes, but I'm only doing about 50 percent of it "right."* In fact, Pat didn't even want to work with Madden at first. And Madden definitely didn't have a life coach to help him slow down and evaluate the opportunity before him in a fresh, new way.

Like John Madden, no one has likely done the same for you (until now).

Remember that time when you got your first big "mentor meeting" with an executive you admired? You worked up the guts to shoot them an email, patiently waited through four rescheduled meetings from their assistant, and finally got the thirty minutes you desperately needed to discover the right path to take you from director to VP. And as you sat there listening to their stories and advice, you were secretly thinking, *Crap, I don't want to do all that.* Maybe it was the three moves their family made so they could chase the big job. Maybe it was the nanny they hired to help shuffle their kids around since they clearly couldn't do that *and* the big job. Maybe the actual roles they took made your spine cringe and your nose turn up ever so slightly. You may have even thought, *Eh, maybe I DON'T want to be a VP.*

Or maybe it was when you got excited to start a side hustle (that you dreamt might even turn into a full hustle). You followed some people on Instagram for years, and you Googled your way to understanding the steps you should take to start hustling. You bought three books on the topic. And then you took the big step of joining a mastermind or online course that was finally the step that screamed, *I'M ACTUALLY GOING TO DO THIS!* You took the course, soaked in the advice, and filled an entire notebook with notes on how to start your hustle. You came up with a name, logo, and maybe even bought a website domain. But then, as you cracked open that notebook full of 100 pages of notes and to-dos: You. Did. Absolutely. Nothing. Paralyzed, you thought, *I know what to do, but I'm never going to be able to be as disciplined as they were and execute ALL of this! Thank you, next.*

Or maybe you are even more like me than I thought. Maybe you quit your sexy, stable, and lucrative job to pursue something new. You knew you had a superpower to coach and speak to people on topics like growing their business and company culture. You even uncovered a secret formula-not-formula . . . say, like using authenticity purposefully and powerfully. On paper, everything told you *should* become a business coach and keynote speaker (and maybe a whisper of *author*). But you knew a million others in that space . . . a million other Hair Dudes, if you will. And you never want to turn into a Hair Dude. So, you (initially) abandoned ship and didn't pursue it.

Just like John Madden almost didn't become a broadcasting legend because he didn't want to follow other people's formulas, I almost didn't pursue what I'm doing now (and loooooooove). And just like Madden and me, *you* are likely leaving *your* legacy on the locker room floor too. You have big ideas and big dreams. But then you think the only path to success is following someone else's path, even if some of it makes you feel icky. No wonder you've abandoned so many of your ideas and dreams!

But if you live by The 50% Rule, every dream, goal, or idea you have only requires you to do and/or follow about half of what others have done. Like John Madden did, *you too* can toss out what you don't like and add your own flair, ideas, and personality to every dream you chase.

Stop *following* someone else's dream and start *snagging* half their dream to craft an entirely new dream altogether.

And here's the best part: The 50% Rule doesn't just make your life better. It will change the game for others around you. Maybe even millions. Maybe even gazillions. When you have the guts to use The 50% Rule, there are likely many others who are sick of the old formula too. They're yearning for something fresh and new . . . more unexpected. Something more fun, authentic, and modern.

In my first book, *You Do You(ish)*, I wrote a chapter on the power of being unexpected: the science behind it and how it triggers something in your brain called a "surprise sequence" that hijacks your brain and makes you stand at attention. When you 50% Rule something, you're inherently making *your* iteration of your career, business, project, etc., more unexpected, thus helping others go from Sleeprunning to Awakerunning.

And once you start to experiment with The 50% Rule and feel even the slightest bit of achievement, it snowballs from there.

After Madden got into his groove, there's no doubt he started to feel empowered to (unconsciously) continue to apply The 50% Rule. For example, one of the reasons Madden didn't want to be a broadcaster was that he had a massive fear of flying (he lost several friends in a plane crash involving his college football team, plus he was also claustrophobic). And broadcasting requires a boatload of flying. Not long into his broadcasting journey, Madden flew to San Francisco for a game, and his fear turned into a full-blown panic attack. As it all came to a head, he thought something like, *If I get off this plane without completely losing my shit, I'll never fly again.*

After that flight, he started taking Amtrak trains to games. However, that was a slow process as he was beholden to the shuffle of public transportation. A few years into his broadcasting career, CBS needed to get him to a location more quickly, so they rented him Dolly Parton's tour bus. That's when it hit him: *I can also do broadcasting travel my own way.* That was the birth of the Madden Cruiser, which quickly became more than a logistical problem solver—both Madden *and* the Madden Cruiser are in the Pro Football Hall of Fame!

Maybe even bigger than Madden's own 50% Rule win, others took notice and were inspired to do things their own way too. Al Michaels once said, "I don't think there's anybody who has made the NFL more interesting, more relevant, and has educated more people about football."

Don't conform to the norm. Transform the norm.

What is one big thing you know you'd be amazing at, but you've abandoned ship because once you got into the thick of things, you felt like it just wasn't for you? Was it the real estate class when they told you that success was all about cold calling? Was it the sales career that felt more like you than doing finance all day, but you hated the way most salespeople approached making a sale? Was it the senior level role that you could crush, but it seems everyone before you all compromised to rise?

I want you to pick just one thing you've avoided and abandoned because it didn't sit well with you and give it another go by using The 50% Rule. I can almost guarantee that it will quickly transform from maddening to magnificent to monumental.

6

Welcome in Your Weaknesses and Your Weird

I ran the hurdles in high school for our track and field team. As a five-foot not-quite-three-inch-tall human, this was a bit ludicrous. My vertical limitation definitely made it more challenging to get over each metal tower of terror. In addition to being short, I wasn't the fastest runner on the team. And Lord knows I'm about the least flexible human on the planet.

But, despite these limitations, I had a great track "career." I certainly wasn't an all-state runner, but I won several races throughout my years in track. I even held my high school's 300-meter hurdles record for a while.

People often asked me why I ran the hurdles, and I never had a good answer . . . until about a year ago. I realized that running the hurdles was part of my Personal Pattern (PP). That is, I chose the hurdles because fewer people ran the hurdles than other races. It was one of the more unusual track races.

When I dug deep into the truth behind this, I realized it was a rationale that's been on repeat for me for much of my life.

It's easier to fumble through the unusual than to compete in the usual.

I don't know when or why it started, but throughout my life, my PP has manifested in several ways. A few examples:

- I selected my undergraduate college based on where most people in my high school *weren't* going.

- Out of approximately 35,000 other students, I was the only person in my undergraduate class who graduated with my degree—a statistics major from the business college.

- My lucky number is thirteen.

- I joined a division in a large company at a time when that division wasn't necessarily the "cool" place to work (and eventually became the company's CEO).

- I only like dancing when or where I'm not supposed to dance. Think: no-go on the discotheque and hell-yes at a team meeting.

- And credit goes to the Universe on this one: I married a man who gave me a last name that makes me the ONLY Erin Hatzikostas in the world. Or at least on the Internet.

Now that I'm a more self-reflective human, I realize that this PP says more about me than just "I'm a deviant." I recognize that constantly having a radar to look past the usual and appreciate the unusual has allowed me to safeguard myself from those nasty Comparison Cramps and Copying Calluses (see page 28 for a refresher) that can so easily sneak up when I'm Sleeprunning through work and life.

The 50% Rule is the compass on my radar. And it can be yours too. Using The 50% Rule as your guide, you inherently upend the usual to embrace the unusual. You no longer sit in a world where grinding it out is the key to success because YOU'RE NOT COPYING WHAT ANYONE ELSE IS DOING. You're running your own race, jumping your own hurdles, dancing where fewer seasoned dancers dance.

Look at what everyone else is doing, then refuse to do more than half of it the same way.

When Alfred was growing up, he was your classic nerd.

After entering kindergarten a year early, and then skipping second grade, he was set up perfectly for all the stereotypes and bullying one would expect a nerdy adolescent to experience during his school years. To add to his nerd pedigree, one day, when Alfred was seven, his parents bought accordion lessons from a door-to-door salesperson, putting arguably the most uncool instrument into the hands of the already-oddest duck in school.

While Alfred didn't resist learning the accordion, he also loved pop music. He would listen to more traditional radio songs only after his parents fell asleep (his mom wasn't a big fan of the language and suggestive topics that come with pop music). His favorite song to play (publicly) on the accordion was "Goodbye Yellow Brick Road," by Elton John. But his nerdiness also secretly drew him to a radio show called *The Dr. Demento Radio Show*, which highlighted unusual artists. Dr. Demento was the first person to give Alfred permission to not do the "usual."

When Alfred was in college, he started to 50% Rule music. He was a DJ at his university and often searched for unusual music. Not too long into his time as a DJ, he quickly took on a nickname: Weird Al.

As you probably know, Weird Al and his iconic music parodies went on to make him famous. He brought something new, not just to odd stations like *The Dr. Demento Radio Show*, but to the mainstream music scene, and he became one of the most successful music artists ever. In fact, he became more famous than some of the artists he parodied!

Weird Al perfectly executed The 50% Rule. He blended pop music with nerdy humor to create something fresh and new. And in a twist of 50% Rule irony, only about half the songs he made were parodies. The other half were 100 percent original.

It's easy to suppress your weaknesses and weirdnesses while Sleeprunning on that treadmill. You get caught up in the "exceed to succeed" game. Instead, you should play the "stand out to succeed" game.

Stop outplaying others and start out-uniquing them.

My friend Shelley Brown is a global keynote speaker and author of *Weird Girl Adventures from A to Z*. Through her work, she asks, "What if weird wasn't weird?" and argues that our "weird" actually brings us all together.

What if *your* weird wasn't weird but rather the thing that helps you stand out? The thing that connects you with others? What if your weirdness is the foundation for bringing something new into the world that others crave? Ask yourself these questions, and maybe write down your answers!

- What quirk of yours have you always been a bit embarrassed by?

- What is something you see that others don't?

- What do you love doing that most people hate to do?

- What are you known for?

- What are two highly juxtaposed things you're good at?

- Where do you think people are yearning for something fresh and new?

When you get soft serve ice cream, what do you order? If you're like most people, it's not vanilla, and it's not chocolate. You order a twist. You prefer a little of this and a little of that. Because, despite chocolate being the best tasting thing on the face of this Earth, it just feels a little one-note, doesn't it? Why would you get that when you can get two things swirled into one?

Another friend of mine, Christina Glickman (author of *Xtra: The Art of Being*), is a fashionista. Her style rivals models' style seen in fancy magazines. In fact, in 2022, she attended Paris

Fashion Week, and a photo was taken of her on the street that was later featured in both *Elle* and *Harper's BAZAAR*.

Whenever I pick her brain on fashion, her number one suggestion is to purposefully not be "matchy-matchy." She loves wearing a pink top and red pants. She highly encourages an Adidas tracksuit to be split up—pairing the jacket with a fancier shirt or pairing the bottoms with a dressier jacket. When I gave my first keynote on The 50% Rule, I took her advice and sported black Adidas track bottoms with a formal leather jacket. Boom.

In many ways, The 50% Rule helps us stop being so matchy-matchy. 'Cause matchy-matchy kind of sucks. It's boring. It's predictable. And it *only* turns out awesome if your matchiness is better than everyone else's matchiness. Which is soooo hard to do.

Instead, like Christina does with her fashion, collect unique things and keep some staples in your closet. Mix your black Adidas tracksuit jacket with your green silk top. Dress up your basic white t-shirt with a fancy tie around your neck. Do this with more than just your outfits. Do this with your meetings. Do this with your job. Do this with your career. Do this with your next project. Do this with your business marketing. Stop being matchy-matchy!

You're already a master mixologist in so many ways. So why can't you do that in your professional life? Why does your profession have to be defined the way everyone else defines it? Why can't your weird passions collide? Who says your weaknesses and weirdnesses can't be the things that bring you, your career, and/or your business onto the workplace Top 40 charts?

And as you keep taking one more step towards out-uniquing others, just keep your Polka Face and do a little yodel to yourself.

7
SWOT Yourself

It was just a few months after I launched my business, and despite having an LLC, website, and logo, I had no clue what my business was actually going to do. I spent most of my time blogging and sharing my favorite podcast episodes with others. I also had some stupid idea about coaching people via text or something like that. I was just a few months removed from my big-girl job as CEO of a nine-figure company, but I was completely lost in how to place down the first few bricks for the foundation of my *own* business.

When what to my blundering eyes should appear, but Amy Porterfield with her course extraordinaire! Like a kid who just saw Santa Claus with a sack full of gifts, I stumbled upon what seemed to be the perfect "gift" for my business. Amy was selling an online course that would teach me every step I needed to take to launch my *own* online course. It was clearly the granddaddy of all courses. Her promise of broad impact—while making money while you slept—was surely the answer to my clueless dreams.

I bought Amy's course, and despite my annoying inability to do anything linearly, I consumed her course like a linear BOSS. I watched the videos, set up the tech, three-hole punched the worksheets into folders, and even highlighted things I thought were most important. Say what?! Who IS this girl? I thought, *Wow, I can follow directions when I really want something. I will succeed at launching my online course because I have the discipline and drive to follow this playbook to fruition.* Gold star for me.

Then the big day arrived—video recording day. Online courses are delivered through a series of pre-recorded videos and then accompanied by a series of worksheets or written instructions/homework for the "student" to put into practice. I blocked off two days to do the recordings and recruited our part-time nanny to be my videographer.

Kaitlyn and I gathered at 8:30 the first morning, and I kicked things off by filling her in on the process Amy had taught. This involved a desk, a script, and a course outline. I was ready. She was ready. "Ok, let's start the first video!" I declared.

As you might imagine, the first go was rough. I stopped the first take about seven seconds in. Then we did it over. And over. And over. Six takes were the charm—Video #1 was done! Things got smoother from there. We got in a groove. We even did one video in one take. By the end of the day, we had finished seven videos, and just under half the course recording was done. Woohoo!

That night, after all the craziness of the day was over, I lay in bed reflecting on Course Recording Day #1. I thought, *Wow, we got a lot done today. I'm so proud of us. Those videos were good . . . wait, but I'm not a "good" kinda person. I actually hate "good." I only like doing things great. CRAP!!!*

As I lay there, what began as pride that I had followed through on the most challenging part of the course playbook quickly turned into fear and regret. As I envisioned myself in the videos I'd done earlier that day, I realized that, while I had given good advice, I did not do one single GREAT video. I didn't give my future "student" anything special. I did the videos just like anyone *normal* would do them. And I hate normal.

Despite leading a company called b Authentic Inc and having a major epiphany earlier that year that I should 50% Rule things, I had gotten completely caught up in Santa's—I mean, Amy Porterfield's—magic formula. Despite having had a highly successful corporate career, paving my own path, making up shit along the way, and leading a massive turnaround by using my authenticity as my strategic weapon, I *still* got suckered into thinking that the only way to do something new was to follow the playbook, 100 percent.

As I lay in bed, I thought more about Amy Porterfield and her royal online course status. Then, almost as if I had a pair of fancy Apple Vision Pros on my face, I suddenly visualized the oldest but most effective strategy tool there is—the SWOT analysis. (If you've never done this age-old strategic planning exercise, SWOT stands for Strengths, Weaknesses, Opportunities, and Threats.)

I had been spending too much time on this SWOT analysis already, I just hadn't realized it. I'd been stuck circling my weaknesses for the last month-plus, thinking about all my Ws: I was so much less methodical than Amy, and I wasn't disciplined enough to write out complete scripts for my videos.

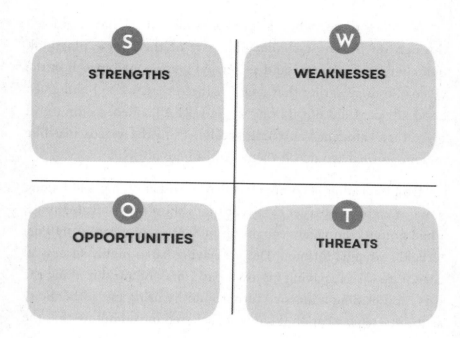

Now I visualized the SWOT matrix and moved myself over one square to the left. I started to think about where my Ss were . . . and maybe where Amy Porterfield's Ws lied. I thought, *While Amy is very disciplined, she's also pretty dull. She even admits that she's not good at improvising or being funny. And those are actually my biggest strengths.*

It hit me: Some of the things in her course playbook weren't there because you had to do them to be successful. They also weren't there because they were the best approach for the people taking your course. They were in the playbook because SHE needed them to succeed. *She* needed a script because she wasn't good at speaking off the cuff. *She* needed a desk in front of her because it made her feel more comfortable. *She* suggested piles of detailed worksheets because that's what people needed for the content *she* delivered.

But that didn't mean it was what was best for me, my content, or my peeps.

Long inhale. Long exhale.

I realized that even though Amy's playbook had given her success, if I replaced some of the guidance that was there to compensate for her weaknesses, it would actually play into my strengths.

And here's the kicker: It would also be better for the people taking my course. If I did things more authentically, my course would be more fun to watch, keep my students' attention longer, AND *DEMONSTRATE* the stuff I was teaching . . . instead of just teaching them!

SWOT away your weaknesses and swoop in your strengths.

With this SWOT analysis not even inked in writing, I realized I had to scrap every one of the videos we recorded earlier that day. Yes, start over. And as much as that *should* have made me feel miserable, it didn't. Because I replaced the dread of the redo with the excitement of anew.

I had an energy and excitement I hadn't felt one iota of in the month leading up to recording the course. I could not wait to re-record the next day. Why? Because I gave myself permission to only do the 50 percent of Amy's course that I liked, I needed, and made sense. I allowed myself to do the other half fully leaning into my own strengths.

I immediately had ideas about how we could make the videos funnier. For example, I thought we could reshoot the first video with me walking down my front walk—all HGTV walk-and-talk style—while Kaitlyn taped her phone to my husband's big, ugly, metal dolly to mimic a big-time camera operation. And we would then show this shot to the students in a video snippet. We would *demonstrate* our humility and authenticity, something taught in the course. I also had a section on taking care of yourself and thought, *What if I recorded that video from our big bathroom tub?!* I lay there laughing, smiling, and giddy about starting over and doing the videos using The 50% Rule.

The following day, Kaitlyn showed up with her coffee and her camera. She didn't even get past our mudroom before I told her about my epiphany and that, oops, we would have to start over.

I'm so proud of the online course we created over those next few weeks. We called it *b Brilliant: From Passed By to Promoted* (you can find it at bit.ly/b-brilliant). I've received so much incredible feedback on it. I even had a Fortune 10 company license it for everyone in their women's Employee Resource Group. Why? Because it's different than anything else they offered; it's relatable and just the kind of no-BS advice they knew their employees needed.

Now, I'm guessing you may have thrown up a weensy bit in your mouth when you saw this whole SWOT analysis thing pop up. I know, I know, the SWOT analysis is corny; it's basically the Olive Garden salad and breadsticks of strategic planning. But in the spirit of The Rule, we will use this semi-tasteless classic in a fresh new way. I want you to adopt SWOT as your new go-to tool when you're feeling some of those nasty Sleeprunning Syndrome symptoms like Comparison Cramps and Self-Doubt Gout.

I want you to take a moment to do a little SWOT analysis of yourself. You'll be a little less strategic and a little more sassy with it, though. If you've never done one before, it's a simple exercise where you make a four-box matrix, like the one on page 68.

Fill it out by starting with your weaknesses (Ws), simply because that's probably your natural tendency and easiest for you to identify.

- What are some things you often struggle with?

- What are the things you hate to do most?

- What scares you?

- What ingrained flaws did your parents hand down to you?

These Ws aren't things to be embarrassed by or even frustrated with. Think of them simply as facts. Can they be changed? Eh, maybe a bit. But these Ws are essentially the cards you're dealt in addition to all the S (Strength) cards you also have.

Now let's move on to those (they're in the first quadrant of the matrix):

- What are the things that come easily to you?

- What do you love doing (especially note things you love but most others hate)?

- What are people always coming to you for?

- What work do you happily work on, even at nine at night when you're in bed?

- What's a secret hidden talent of yours?

- What do you do on your "best day"?

Place these strengths proudly and boldly in the S box.

Next, move on to the Threats box. (And yes, we're working non-linearly. Go figure.) With the Ts for this exercise, I suggest you focus on the past and then look forward.

- What "threats" have you at least perceived because of your "weaknesses"?

- What did your Ws make you hold back from pursuing?

- Which friend do you often compare yourself to because of *their* Ss. What's *your* S that's *their* W?

- Where did you assume you'd fail?

- What relationships were affected by trying to hide or cover up your Ws?

- Looking forward, what one thing will you lose out on if you keep dwelling on your weaknesses?

- How often are you dwelling on your weaknesses publicly, and what negative impact does that have? On you? On others?

And finally, now that you've had your T exorcism, move left again to your Opportunities box. Considering your strengths and The 50% Rule, what opportunities do you have?

- What can you now think about pursuing that you have held back on previously?

- How could you make that dreadful project you're leading more fun by 50% Ruling it, replacing the weaknesses of the typical playbook with your strengths?

- How would your next conversation with your boss change if you 50% Ruled your one-on-ones?

- What innovative new product would you launch into the world if you threw out 50 percent of the stuff you feel is weak and replaced it with 50 percent strengths that other people need?

SWOT Analysis

STRENGTHS

What are the things that you effortlessly ace? The stuff you enjoy doing, even if it's not everyone's cup of tea. What work do you happily tackle, even when it's 9:00 at night and you're lounging in bed? We all have those secret hidden talents, so come on, spill the beans!

WEAKNESSES

What are the things that trip you up? What tasks do you absolutely despise? What gives you the creeps? And let's not forget those lovely genetic flaws inherited from dear old mom and dad. Let's get real and dive into our own flaws and fears.

OPPORTUNITIES

What ideas have you been putting on the backburner? How would your next conversation with your boss change if you 50% Ruled your one-on-ones? What game-changing opportunities are you leaving behind?

THREATS

What scares you the most? Have you ever felt insecure because of your flaws? Ever felt envious of a friend because they have something you don't see in yourself? Did you ever think you would fail?

Start small. Pick one thing—a project, a relationship, a meeting—that you can experiment with, implementing the results of your SWOT analysis in the next few weeks. And then simply observe the crap out of every step you take. Watch others' reactions. Check in on how you're feeling along the way. Wean yourself off the satisfaction of Sleeprunning through the playbook you think you *should* follow. Start getting addicted to the new feelings you have. Blast some music as you do it. Dance in your bathtub. Get addicted. Observe the magic.

REAL PEEPS STORY
....

POOH-POOH POWERPOINT

When Jen DeSantis got the email that a senior leader in her company wanted to meet with her, she was excited. Jen was new in her marketing role at the company, but she'd been in marketing for a long time. She knew that business leaders often don't fully understand or value what the marketing team does.

Even though the meeting was called with little time to prepare, her immediate reaction was to create a fancy PowerPoint presentation. Much like you probably do, she thought that if it's not in a fancy "deck," it's not real. Also, because she was meeting with someone more senior, there was this gravitational pull to create a formal presentation. Jen said, "I felt I had to prove myself since my role is new." PowerPoint felt like her best path to proving her worth and the value that marketing brought to the leader overall.

But then Jen paused and did something insanely simple but critical to enacting The 50% Rule. She thought about what *she* would want if she was on the other side of that meeting. She realized that she wouldn't want to flip through some fancy PowerPoint. Instead, she'd like to have an in-depth discussion focused on enhancing their partnership and their work together. Jen said, "A usual approach would have been to follow the norm and make a pretty presentation, spending HOURS or DAYS to impress a senior leader. Since hearing about The 50% Rule, I have taken that to heart—thinking about role reversal and what I would want + time spent, and whether that demonstrates value."

The meeting was a huge success. Jen recalled, "The senior leader LOVED the conversation. She opened up about some key projects and initiatives she wanted to start. She referred people to me as a strategic partner to bring into the fold on projects. I've now been brought in early to strategic planning versus being an afterthought."

Jen was able to work an important mind-muscle that The 50% Rule helps strengthen. That is, value is not "counted" by the number of things you produce. Value is determined by how much you focus on producing the optimal outcome. Jen reflected on the meeting and how knowing The 50% Rule changed her approach: "With The 50% Rule, I find I am more me, being more authentic in what I do, not what I assume would be expected."

....

Hùng Phạm and his colleagues had been round and round the internal approval mulberry bush more times than they could count. Hùng was working for a biotech company, and they needed a go/no-go decision on a U.S.-based pilot for an app they had developed. As is customary in most large or highly regulated companies, decisions like these don't lie in just one person or department's hands; they need the support of leaders from several teams.

Hùng says, "We had done the requisite dog and pony show many times. To support the 'show,' we developed PowerPoint decks. Lots of them. But we worked tirelessly to make sure they were scaled down to critical information for the audience."

After multiple rounds of meetings, his team was told that their final step was to get an official decision from their U.S. Leadership Team (USLT). After waiting weeks to find a time when the Grand Pooh-bahs could all gather, the final meeting was set. On a Tuesday. At 7:45 a.m.

Hùng went on, "Since my Global counterparts and I had already been doing the dog and pony show, we could have easily taken a slide from here, a slide there, and—BAM—collated a new PowerPoint without a lot of effort. However, as much as I enjoy fiddling with PowerPoint, I realized I had presented to and been in the room for USLT presentations. In those meetings, the participants rarely pre-read the PowerPoint, or worse, they asked the presenter to 'get on with it.' Bottom line: We needed to provide only the essential information the USLT needed to make a decision. Nothing more. Nothing less."

So, instead of culling down the previous PowerPoint presentations, or adding an executive summary, Hùng had an idea to 50% Rule their final meeting: "We're going to write a memo!" he said in an email. "And we're going to keep it to only two pages."

The team got to work. They spent several hours discussing and debating what information was most critical. In places where they determined more detail might be needed, they kept it "on hand" and simply referenced that backup information was available.

Hùng knew this approach was VERY different (ok, half-different?) than standard company protocol. So, to be sure people didn't miss the memo (literally!), he not only attached it to the invite but also sent separate emails to each of the USLT members individually, attaching the memo again and reminding them of his request to review it before their meeting.

Tuesday at 7:45 arrived. When everyone joined the call, Hùng asked, "Did you get a chance to read the memo?" Every single USLT member chimed in: *Nope*. ARGH! Hùng recalls the moment: "Taking a second to muster up my courage, I said, 'Let me resend it, so it's top of your queue. We can take five minutes to read it. Then we'll have our discussion.' Instead of trying to go through a huge PowerPoint document, the entire group sat silently on a Microsoft Teams call, reading the memo."

After the five minutes were up, instead of Hùng presenting anything, he simply asked, "What are your concerns?" The group spent no more than fifteen minutes talking things through before they got their official approval! Because Hùng and his colleagues had spent so much time 50% Ruling the information to ensure it could fit on a two-page memo, the meeting was the most effective and efficient meeting they held throughout the entire process.

"We got our 'go' approval by bucking the system. The 50% Rule helped us stop and think more about what people needed versus what we thought was required. And, when you do that, things tend to go your way . . . and, more importantly, quickly!"

8

Tradition Shmadition

When Whitney Houston finished exhaling that final line, ". . . and the home . . . of the . . . brave . . ." it felt like the entire stadium was vibrating. You knew you had just witnessed the best performance ever of "The Star-Spangled Banner." Whitney's performance at the 1991 Super Bowl is forever etched in the hearts, minds, and souls of nearly every spectator who witnessed it. I'm guessing you were one of those souls. But it's likely you don't know the story behind that iconic moment.

For over 175 years, the National Anthem was sung and played with largely the same tempo and beats. Bands and singers could perform it in their sleep. And fans likely often *fell* asleep when they heard it.

But Whitney wanted to mix it up. She didn't want to do this to "show off" her singing prowess; she wanted to do it because she knew people needed it. Whitney said, "We were in the Gulf War at the time. It was an intense time for our country. A lot of our daughters and sons were overseas fighting. I could see in the stadium, I could see the fear, the hope, the intensity, the prayers going up."

She recognized that singing a song mainly as an exercise in futility wasn't enough. The song needed to be sung in a way that brought energy and inspiration to everyone listening. This idea, however, was not met with open arms. Executives at both the NFL and CBS, the network doing the Super Bowl telecast, pushed back. As her music director Rickey Minor put it, "Change is one of the most constant things that happens, yet we resist something foreign to us."

In a way, the resistance was understandable. This was, in fact, the nation's cherished anthem. It's a song to honor our country and the servicepeople who protect it. It's meant to be a symbol of unity and patriotism. It's serious. It's sacred. It's symbolic. But that doesn't mean it has to be the same.

Altering tradition isn't a sign of disrespect. Altering it allows us to inject it with the relevance of the present, to greater effect.

Whitney and her manager resisted the executives' pushback. It wasn't that Whitney was going to 100 percent change "The Star-Spangled Banner." She didn't change any of the words. She didn't sing it while swinging from the rafters. She 50% Ruled it. She changed the tempo a bit and made it more jazzy. She infused it with more passion . . . passion she thought others needed to hear.

The executives finally, reluctantly, agreed. In fact, although they said "Yes," they made her record it and perform it lip-synced juuuuust to be sure she didn't go rogue. (Yep, Whitney's performance wasn't live.)

And the rest is history. Literally. Not only was her rendition a mind-blowingly beautiful and powerful moment, but her willingness to 50% Rule the anthem forever changed the song. When was the last time you were at an event and heard it? You likely don't disengage (like you do when the flight attendant does their safety talk). You listen. You wait to hear just how they'll make it their own. You "ooh" and "ahh" when someone nails it.

If Whitney hadn't had the vision and the guts to push forward her more inspirational version of the anthem, you might still be listening to the same song, different century. Rather than putting your hand on your heart, you'd reach for your phone. Instead of singing along, you'd think about what to make for dinner. Instead of leaning in, you'd tune out.

But it wasn't just the music Whitney changed. Whitney also didn't perform the song in a dress or business suit. She sang the anthem while wearing a white tracksuit and headband. Again, this wasn't to be all *look at me*. She was there to watch the big game, and she sure as hell didn't want to watch the game in a flippin' dress.

Now, this may not sound like a big deal in this post-COVID, leggings-are-a-woman's-best-friend era. But in 1991, this was another example of her bucking the norm and 50% Ruling her appearance. She not only gave every future singer permission to do the anthem their own way, but she also gave them permission to dress their own way. Sometimes when you 50% Rule small shit, you accidentally change the trajectory of big shit.

Whitney's story demonstrates how you can take The 50% Rule, put a tracksuit on it, and turn it into more than an antidote to your Sleeprunning ailments. You might start by applying The Rule to add a little flair or even make yourself feel better. In doing so, you very well could change how something is done . . . forever.

Sometimes when you 50% Rule small shit, you accidentally change the trajectory of big shit.

Whitney didn't know how significant an impact her 50% Ruling would be. She didn't know that her decision, founded on changing things to better others' lives, would lead to innovation. Whitney didn't say, "I want to be the Chief Innovation Officer of 'The Star Spangled Banner.'" Innovation doesn't come out of a boardroom. It doesn't come from a line of code in a Fortune 500 company's system. It doesn't come from a billion-dollar investment. Innovation comes from the individual, bold moves that humans take every day as they prioritize what's needed over what's normal.

When you trust your authenticity (or your guts) to prioritize what's needed over what's normal it'll likely change the trajectory of, not just Future You, but the future for others, and that's when things get REAL interesting. The 50% Rule will always be the best probiotic to keep your guts healthy and humming . . . to a whole new tune.

• • • • • • • • • • • • •

Innovation comes from the
individual, bold moves that
humans take every day as they
prioritize what's needed over
what's normal.

• • • • • • • • • • • • •

9

Don't Throw the Baby Out with the Hot Tub Water

It was 1999, and I was a few years into my corporate career. I had been hired into Aetna's Actuarial program, which selected ten to fifteen people each year to rotate through various actuarial jobs while also studying for the requisite actuarial exams.

The good news? I was flourishing in my jobs. The bad news? I was failing in my exams.

Despite not being able to pass an actuarial exam to save my life, I was in the program for my second year and was placed into an area called Service Pricing and Stop Loss. Sounds sexy, doesn't it? The group was mostly a band of misfits, with the average team member being three decades older than me.

But there was this one guy, Manny, who was about my age and seemed pretty cool. I didn't know him well (he was Service Pricing, I was Stop Loss), but we got to know each other over time. Okay, truth be told, we mostly got to know each other because I was given a programming assignment, and I had NO idea how to program. So, I asked this nice guy in Service Pricing to help me. He just *happened* to be cute.

About nine months into my rotation, my friends and I were gearing up for our annual ski trip to Vermont. My father loved to brag to his buddies about our trip. He'd say to them, "It's amazing. Erin and her friends organize a ski trip every year, and each person gets lodging, ski tickets, food, and beer for only about twenty-five dollars per person. Wanna know how they do it? Twenty-five people in a three-bedroom house!"

While I may have gotten a tiny bit email-flirty with this Manny dude, I remember thinking, *He's our age and pretty cool. At a minimum, he should hang out with my friends.* I invited him to go on our next ski trip, and he said yes.

Friday night, we arrived and began doing what twenty-five-year-old-ish people do: play drinking games. About two hours into our never-ending game of flip-cup, Manny and his wingman arrived. It was clear we weren't in the office anymore, and we spent the next few hours getting to know each other outside of cubicle walls and Excel macros.

At some point, socially lubricated, I asked him if he wanted to get into the hot tub. I remembered seeing a sauna and hot tub in the basement, and for some reason, no one else had yet taken advantage of these amenities (flip-cup *is* alluring).

We went to the basement, where the hot tub and sauna were in a separate, dimly lit room. To get changed into our bathing suits, I went into that separate room while Manny changed in the larger basement room. We then both went into the hot tub and talked for a while, and eventually, I leaned over (yes, me) and kissed him. I remember feeling like hot shit. I kissed the hottest guy in Service Pricing and Stop Loss. Take that, actuarial exams.

Fast forward about four months, and Manny and I were still dating. We had taken our romance beyond the cubicle chats and hot tub hangout. It was May, and we were talking about going to the beach that weekend when Manny said, "Are you going to wear your blue bathing suit?" I thought, *Holy crap, most men don't remember what you wore yesterday, let alone four months ago!* He then elaborated, "The one you were wearing in the hot tub? Inside out. With the brown part showing."

I almost passed out but managed to reply, "Are you kidding me?! I was wearing my top inside out in that hot tub the whole time, and you never told me?!" To which he responded matter-of-factly, "I didn't want to embarrass you."

Here's the thing: If you throw out *everything* that is standard practice or guidance, it's like putting on your bathing suit in a dimly lit room. While you think you might be hot shit, you're sure to have a mishap. You'll likely do something backward. You may even make an ass of yourself. Others' input *is* valuable. It gives you some light. There is value in the 50% you keep.

When I launched my first book, it was only available as a paperback or e-book, but I wanted to do an audiobook as well. Creating an audiobook was a strategic imperative. Plus, I love love love doing new stuff. I'm a starter. I crave exponential learning. I revel in proving to myself that I can do totally new things.

So, about six months after releasing my book, I started pulling together the audiobook version. I looked at a myriad of production options and decided to hire a referral from a referral from a friend. Yes, basically a total stranger. He was local, though, and I liked his demeanor.

In true Midwestern-born fashion, I invited this stranger into my home to begin recording the audiobook. After casing the joint, we landed on the basement as the best acoustical place to do the recording. Spoiler alert ('cause I know what you're thinking): I did NOT end up on *Dateline*, despite my doing an excellent job of setting up the plot. The good news is that he turned out to just be an audio producer and not a serial killer looking to off me in my basement. But I digress.

Steve and I settled into my basement, and I immediately spewed out all the reasons I hate audiobooks. I talked to him about the fact that I preach the power of authenticity every day— and damn it to hell if I'm going to do this audiobook inauthentically. I went on (likely quite annoyingly by now) about how most authors put me to sleep . . . that they're basically trying to "act" but sound like someone reading the Gettysburg Address.

Now, Steve is *also* not a conformist. He spends most of his days and evenings doing sound for organizations like the NFL and World Wrestling Entertainment (WWE). Despite the perceived sexiness of these organizations, Steve was mostly confined to an audio box. So, as I got more and more fired up about my newfound desire to do my audiobook my own way, he just about jumped on the couch in a Tom Cruise-on-*Oprah* moment, ready to be the holder as I kicked the normal audiobook process through the goalposts and out of the frickin' stadium. Grrrrrrrr—let's goooo!

We devised the most creative and audacious strategy you could imagine. First of all, I was NOT going to read the book word for word (that's so inauthentic!). Instead, I was going to talk off the cuff about each chapter, highlighting the most salient story and/or points. We knew this did not adhere to Audible content guidelines. But who needed them? They only dominate the audiobook market.

We were so jacked up and stupid that we saw that as an opportunity. We could market the book as so authentic that Audible wouldn't even allow it. "F*ck Audible" signs were being ideated. We were excited, thrilled, and ready to blow up and reshape the audiobook market completely. You know, 'cause I'm so famous and influential that I could make this happen.😑

We outlined our strategy further and walked away that day with a plan for a non-plan. When we got together the next time, we would blow shit up, and it would be epic.

But.

I was at least smart enough to bring our ideas back to my #1 right-hand person on the b Authentic Inc team. Rachel had been working with me, supporting the growth of b Authentic Inc, for over two years at that point. So I thought, *Ehhh, maybe I should just run this little plan by Rachel before we hit* Go. Rachel also happens to be an audiobook junkie, so maybe she would have something to say about something. Of course, I expected that something to be like, "Hell to the yes, Erin, go for it! I love you always being authentic. You go, girl."

Except that wasn't *exactly* how our conversation went. I jumped on a call and started pouring out all my "great," 100 percent authentic ideas to Rachel. When I finally paused to hear her encouraging feedback, she simply stated, "I'd be fucking pissed." Exact quote.

She went on to tell me that if she bought an audiobook and didn't get the actual . . . book, she would be angry. And also,

Rachel said, even though some authors are boring, she loves to listen to them read their work in their own voice. She calmed many of my other fears but also quickly reminded me that you *can* go too far with your authenticity. Kicking shit 100 percent out of the stadium may feel fun, but it's likely not good for anybody but you.

Beware: Your love affair with 100%ing may flare others with despair.

While much of this book so far has focused on the 50 percent you usher in, it's just as important that you acknowledge and honor 50 percent of what's already out there. It's essential to learn from others.

For example, when I started my business, if I had just slowed my roll for a few months, I would have pumped the brakes on surface-level stuff like creating a logo, and instead hired a coach who specialized in the business model I wanted to build. I would have doubled the hours I listened to podcasts. Or sought out people who were doing the things I wanted to do. I would have saved so much time and money. Instead, I spent the first year fumbling around like an idiot, working on all kinds of stupid little stuff I *thought* I had to do to succeed rather than hiring a coach who would help me focus on the few big things that were critical to early success.

You must seek out others' advice and counsel, many of whom have gone down hellish paths which they're more than willing to make sure you don't head down. People who've worked at your company since what feels like the Dinosaur Age do actually know some important stuff. Even if someone seems like a total stuck-in-the-mud, *some* of what they tell you is really important to know. You're crazy not to seek out their advice. Find a good playbook. Pay for an online course. Talk to mentors. Listen to podcasts. Hire a coach. Read books. Tune into Mom. Then take *some* of it. Not all of it. About 50 percent of it.

But please, don't throw the baby out with the hot tub water. Don't create something totally crazy new because you hate the way it was done before. Other people might like it. They probably like about half of the way it was done before. If Whitney Houston had stepped into that stadium and sang "Yankee Doodle" or even "Greatest Love of All," despite the latter arguably being one of the greatest songs of all time, most people would have been fucking pissed. I'm sure Rachel would have been.

If you're the kind of person that is a bit of a rebel without a pause, here are some questions to ask yourself next time you feel yourself going 100 percent rogue:

- What do I like about how other people do things? What do I not like?

- Is there one thing that seems like it's critical to do, even if it feels a bit meh?

- What is the intent/goal of the "normal" process? How can I preserve that intent but reach it using a slightly different approach?

- What about the current way of doing things is important for the end customer/recipient/user?

- What if I do the normal process for X but I call it something slightly different? Does that make it feel more like me? Small name changes often unlock your permission to apply The

50% Rule (e.g., I have to write a "summary" at the top of my CV, but what if I call it "Keys to My Success" instead?).

If I had gone totally rogue with my audiobook, I would have probably broken the record for the highest Audible return percentage. Yeah, that's not a record I am looking to break. I was just overruling the guidelines to compensate for what I hated about audiobooks. The problem was that I hadn't also thought about what that would have done for most people who like audiobooks (otherwise, why would they be buying them?!).

And where did I land? At 50 percent-ish, of course. I ended up reading the entire book. But I did a few things my own way too. For example, when we were recording the requisite opening for the book, I noticed that some authors put a little music behind their boring reading. It made it, well, a little less boring. When I proposed that idea to Steve, he grimaced and went on and on about potential copyright issues and how using others' music might be an issue, blah, blah.

Instead of being annoyed with his response, I looked over at the ridiculously overpriced, used-three-times, American Girl keyboard my daughter had abandoned in the basement and said, "Fine. I'll just record an original 'score.'" And no, I have zero keyboard skills. Instead, I played random keys and giggled while reading my stupid, required opening thing. I hoped it would make a few others laugh too.

I also didn't completely abandon my idea to do a more authentic "reading" of each chapter. Instead of this idea of fully replacing the reading, though, I decided to add it at the end. For each of the twenty-nine chapters of the book, Steve interviewed me about each chapter, and I gave one key story or point from that chapter, plus one reflection or action the listener could take to implement that point. We called them "Chapter Quick Fixes" and recorded them in both audio and video. By doing this, I could also use some videos for my Authenticity Challenge "course." Take that, Amy Porterfield. And Audible.

Here's the hard truth I need to whack you with: Authenticity is not actually about you.

Authenticity is exposing who you are, when people least expect it, in the service of others.

Authenticity is about doing the things that sometimes feel hard, off-script, not normal, vulnerable, or different. But doing them for others. Doing them to create connection, increase trust, engage, excite, and motivate.

As soon as you start to veer too far off course, there's a good chance you're over-dialing your authenticity button. You're kicking things out of the end zone, but probably not *through* the goalposts. The ball might feel good coming off your foot, but you're probably shanking it to the left or right. And nobody likes a shanker. Don't be a shanker.

Sidenote: I may have failed all my actuarial exams, but I passed my husband exam. Manny and I have been happily married (more than 50 percent of the time!) for twenty years, and he's now seen me in WAY more embarrassing situations than an inside-out bathing suit.

10

It's Your Job(s) to Collect More Dots

I'll never forget the day I graduated with my MBA. I told Manny—and I quote—"If I ever talk about taking another class for a grade, lock me in a closet and throw away the key." I knew it wasn't the learning part I hated. If you ask me why I left my executive job to start something totally new, the primary reason was that I love to learn exponentially. But grad school was so structured and littered with playbooks that later on, I felt like I had hit the same wall as I did in my corporate job.

While I have 0.0 regrets about making the leap from corporate CEO to author, professional speaker, and coach-sultant, what I know now that I wish I'd known then is that I could have done more exponential learning in corporate than I thought.

It's easy to get caught up in the traditional education system, formal degrees, and certificates. It's easy to use a step stool to hop on the professional hamster wheel and take all your company-prescribed LinkedIn Learning courses and leadership modules so you can do the job better.

But remember the problem with focusing too much on doing "better" than your peers? If that's all you do, then you'll always be trying to outwork the next person. You'll always be running yourself into the ground. If you went to college and got a big fat degree, but then spend the rest of your career only riding the corporate training trolley, that's equivalent to being the valedictorian of your class and then living in your parents' basement until you're thirty-eight.

You probably know that Steve Jobs never finished college. Still, you may not know that shortly after Jobs dropped out of college, he decided to audit a calligraphy class (i.e., he didn't take the class to get credit towards his degree; he took it simply because he was interested in the topic) at the same college he'd just formally bagged. In his famous 2005 Stanford commencement speech, Jobs credits this calligraphy class for the beauty of Apple's distinct typography. When he took the class, he didn't intend to use the things he learned to improve his career or business. But in hindsight, this random class contributed to creating one of the most iconic brands ever.

It is your job to continually seek out new knowledge, material, ideas, and experiences for *your* half of the 50 percent. These things won't fall into your lap on a Tuesday afternoon while attending your fifth Zoom meeting of the day. They aren't handed down to you in Aunt Betty's will. They're not delivered to your door in an Amazon package you ordered while taking your morning poopy.

While I was recently working on a marketing project for our podcast, someone mentioned the book *Oversubscribed: How to Get People Lining Up to Do Business with You* by Daniel Priestley. I picked it up and read it more quickly than anything I'd read in years. Here's the thing: I first consumed the content to help grow my business. But I quickly began to let my mind wander and realized that a few of the concepts he teaches added incredible fuel to what I teach regarding authenticity. A few weeks after finishing the book, I infused those new concepts into a sales training I did for a Fortune 250 company. The training was a MASSIVE success, with one leader declaring at the end, "We've done a lot of sales training over the last two to three years, but this was definitely the best one." The head honcho guy even mentioned that he attended the live two-hour event, and then he watched the entire thing again the next week!

That is the power of continuous learning—you never know what you will find. You have to get out there. You have to get curious. You have to invest a bit. You have to attend a conference your company doesn't pay for. You need to talk to people in different industries. You need to read books and listen to podcasts. You must become a collector—not of stamps or baseball cards—but of perspectives, ideas, and experiences.

Your job doesn't define this.

Your role doesn't define this.

Even your future desires don't necessarily define this.

Because the best things often don't come from IKEA with an assembly manual. They come from somewhere you least expect them, and are only built from curiosity, inspiration, and motivation (and not a damn little Allen wrench).

Ted Lasso quickly became one of my favorite shows of all time. If you haven't yet watched it, start watching it ASAP or we can't be friends. Sorry, it's that good.

When its star and executive producer Jason Sudeikis was interviewed on the *Men In Blazers* podcast, the host asked him about the influences that led him to create something as unique as *Ted Lasso*. Jason talked about a time when he became enthralled with British shows, old and new. TiVo had just come out, so he could record and watch things he had traditionally been too busy working to see.

He started watching the original U.K. *Office* and Sacha Baron Cohen's *Da Ali G Show*. He would watch these shows in awe, wondering how they pulled off such unique feats. He also discovered *Monty Python and the Holy Grail* around the same time. It was the twenty-fifth anniversary of the movie, and a friend took him to see it in the theater. He couldn't believe he had never watched it before. "This is everything I love. How am I not influenced by this? [It] just challenged any sort of arrogance that I would have had about comedy and just everything I thought was possible or that I thought was good. This has been sitting here for years, and I wasn't influenced by it until that very moment. And then I just realized, *Oh, I got a lot to learn.*"

Jason admits that this perplexed him since, at that time, he was working at The Second City, one of the most prestigious comedy programs in the world. He was learning from the best of the best. He thought he was at the top of his learning mountain.

Although Jason was working at one of the most well-known improv theaters, it was actually these British comedy influences that he stumbled upon in his *personal* life—things he simply was following out of passion, not a specific purpose—that most profoundly impacted the trajectory of his career, and ultimately the unforgettable work he did in creating *Ted Lasso*.

This realization, of course, could only be seen in hindsight. As Jobs once said, "You can't connect the dots looking forward; you can only connect them looking backward. So you have to trust that the dots will somehow connect in your future."

Collect lots of dots.
Then, let them plot their own slots.

Or, as Ted Lasso once asked, "What do you get when you mix a rhinoceros with an elephant? . . . El-eph-I-know." So get out there, mix up some rhinos with some elephants, and see where it goes.

SECTION 3:

· · · · · · · · · · · · · ·

50% YOUR LEADERSHIP

11

Punt the Ball

"Ella, for the love of God, stop being a slob and clean your room!" My daughter is sixteen years old, and despite her being a really great kid, her bedroom can become a full-on disaster. I used to scream something like that at her on a regular basis. Until the day she said what I should have known all along. "When you tell me to clean my room, I don't want to do it. But when I get inspired on my own, I love cleaning it."

This was certainly true. When she gets the urge to clean, she doesn't just pick things up—she organizes, labels, and color-codes. Her room goes from university fraternity house to Marie Kondo perfection in a hot second. In fact, it happens so under the radar that I usually don't even see it transpire.

I used to be massively selfish with The 50% Rule. First, I kept it to myself as my own personal pet for years. Then, I began to blurt it out for others to use—often helping them get unstuck from a problem they were wrestling with. I thought I was being so giving, blessing others as I'd been blessed. I was letting them in on the little hack I'd been secretly using to do big shit while also doing everything with more fervor, flair, and fun than everyone else around me.

I realized that The 50% Rule is also the best tool to motivate others, freeing you from the binary of keeping your nose entirely out of people's business (like I started to have to do with my daughter and her pigsty room) and fully prescribing every action a person should take. I realized The Rule can take you well beyond curing your Sleeprunning Syndrome. It can be the ultimate doctor *and* coach to help you motivate others to take action, innovate, and achieve big things. If you commit to using The 50% Rule as a leadership tool, you'll help propel your team, colleagues, and kids through a simple mindset shift of their brain.

In this next section, we'll Marie Kondo The 50% Rule to transform it from a lonely, self-interested propeller to a leadership weapon that will help you motivate your team, colleagues, and maybe even your slobby teenager.

12

This Ain't Just Therapy

For over five years, I've been completely and utterly obsessed with authenticity. I did a TEDx Talk on it, wrote my first book on the topic, and spoke to and worked with forty-plus companies and organizations about it. But here's the truth: For the first three and a half years, I was basically making shit up.

Yes, I had my own lived experience. And I researched and reflected on many other authentic people and experiences to help craft my message. But I didn't have cold, hard proof that what I was preaching would help anyone else achieve tangible, positive results.

That all changed in 2021 when my team and I launched a first-of-its-kind, national research study on the impact of authenticity in the workplace. We wanted to know what tangible benefits could be quantified from workplaces, leaders, and people who practiced authenticity more than the inauthentic bozo next door.

My team is definitely not composed of a bunch of academic researchers. So, we partnered with smart research people at

Material[1] to craft, launch, and analyze a legit study. We didn't wing this; we ensured that we conducted an entirely credible, unbiased survey to collect the data. Our hypothesis was that authenticity has tangible, positive benefits to people in the work environment. What we didn't expect was the enormity of its impact. Some things we learned . . .

1. **People respect authority, but they follow authenticity:** We asked people if their manager was authentic. Then, several questions later, we asked them if they would follow their manager if they took a job elsewhere. People with authentic managers were six times more likely to follow their manager. Said another way, you'll enjoy 600 percent greater followership if you are authentic. And duh, it's easy to extrapolate how this would be true for more than if you're someone's manager. When you're posting on social media, more people will follow you. When you're leading a cross-functional project, more people will do the stuff you want them to do. When you ask your kid or partner to do something, they're a helluva lot more likely to listen and follow your lead if you're authentic. Authenticity is like wearing a multi-colored, flowered suit in a sea of navy-blue suits. It feels a bit weird, but in the end, you

---

1. To pull together "The Impact of Authenticity in the Workplace" study, we partnered with Material, a leading global consumer intelligence and customer experience consultancy, to develop a custom, twenty-four-question "Workplace Survey." We then worked with Momentive's SurveyMonkey Audience to collect the data. Information on how respondents are recruited to SurveyMonkey is available at surveymonkey.com/mp/find-survey-participants/. On January 29, 2022, we sent the survey to working adults (full-time or part-time employed people) in the United States. We received 1,122 completed responses by the end of that same day. The total sample has a margin of error of +/- 2.985 percent. Lastly, we worked again with Material to analyze and present the results contained in this report. Yes, it was one big research party . . . and we all ate the cake.

will be the one everyone talks about and wants to be around.

2. **Authenticity is a fast pass to creating trust:** We also asked people how often authenticity was practiced within their company. We gave them a Likert scale (fancy research words for a five-point scale): always, usually, sometimes, rarely, never. Then, in another question, we asked them to answer "Yes" or "No" to the statement *There is a high level of trust within my company*. People who work at highly authentic companies were found to respond "Yes" to this trust statement four times more than companies whose culture was less authentic. People walk around with trust-o-meters buzzing at all times. And when their meter is green (i.e., they trust you), amazing things will happen!

3. **You get better results for yourself:** When we did this study, we weren't just interested in the greater good. We also wanted to know how everyday people might benefit from being more authentic. We asked people a simple question: *Can you be authentic at work?* For those who answered "Yes," we then asked if they could attribute the fact that they were authentic directly to any of the several things we listed. We found, for example, that 52 percent attributed their manager's confidence in them to their authenticity. 30 percent directly attributed a promotion or pay increase to their authenticity. And 45 percent attributed their job security to their authenticity at work.

• • • • • • • • • • • • •

Authenticity is like wearing a
multi-colored, flowered suit in
a sea of navy-blue suits. It
feels a bit weird, but in the
end, you will be the one
everyone talks about and
wants to be around.

• • • • • • • • • • • • •

We learned so much more than this too. If you want to geek out and dive fully into the study's results (or just passive aggressively send it to your shitty, phony boss/teammate/colleague), you can download a copy of the full report at bauthenticinc.com/research.

While the direction of the results didn't surprise us, the *magnitude* of the positive benefits blew us away.

Here's the thing: Authenticity is essentially like that moment when birthday cake is served at a little kid's party. The kids finish their activities, and the parents come around with the cake and ice cream. Kids are eager to grab their rightful piece. Many even ask for a bigger piece or more ice cream. Then, when the kids are done being served, the hosts wander around the perimeter wall of parents. They ask each parent if *they* want a piece of cake. And what do most parents say? . . . "No, thank you." But what are most parents thinking? *I really want a piece of cake.*

That's authenticity. Everyone craves it. Few have the courage to dish it or take it.

So, eat the damn cake.

13

Stop F*cking People Up

"Don't fucking do it." It was as succinct a response as you could get. But it certainly wasn't the response I was expecting . . . or hoping for.

For several months, my mind had been circulating around this notion that it was time for me to do something new. After twenty-two years at the same large Fortune 50 company, I felt like it was time to jump ship and do something totally different. It wasn't because I was burnt out or unhappy. In fact, I had just led a major turnaround as CEO of one of their subsidiary companies and was having (relatively) good fun doing it.

Instead, at this point, I had become fully self-aware of another one of my Personal Patterns.

My PP went like this: I got a new role. I quickly became overwhelmed and exhausted at how much I didn't know and had to learn. I worked hard to overcome these challenges. I became the go-to person. Work was easy. I became uninspired (I *used* to think I was just getting lazy). I yearned for something new. I hated that I wanted something new. I realized I was most motivated and inspired by new challenges and exponential learning. I got a new role. Repeat.

As I became increasingly aware of my PP, rather than refusing to dance with this stranger, I started doing the two-step with it. When this latest PP popped up again, I had a feeling that the exponential learning and challenge I was looking for might not come from the place that had been my dance floor over the last three decades.

As I kicked around ideas for what that new challenge might be, it quickly felt like I was heading on a long drive on the foggiest of days. Should I look for a CEO position at a smaller, start-up(ish) company, or maybe I should consult or start my own company? I didn't know the answer. But I did see the power of getting advice from others.

Around the same time, a former coworker came back into my life. He was working for a company we were potentially going to partner with. I wasn't sure what he'd been up to since he left my dance floor, so I stalked him on LinkedIn. I quickly noticed he had dabbled in many of the "buckets" I was considering. He'd worked for a start-up, done his own consulting, and worked for several large companies. I thought, *Joe[2] is the perfect person to kick this secret idea around with and get advice from.*

I reached out to Joe, and we jumped on a call the following week. I admit, I was a bit nervous; this was the first time I was going to speak out loud what I had been (safely) floating in my head for months. When we connected, I spent a solid five minutes bringing him up to speed, explaining why I thought it might be time to move on. Then I told him some ideas about what I

---

2. Name has been changed.

might want to do next. I told him how I was excited to hear his thoughts and guidance since he had seemingly dabbled in all the facets I was considering.

That's when he barely took a breath and uttered those stunning words, "Don't fucking do it."

I was shocked. How could every other path I was exploring be that deplorable of an idea that it was that simple (and disappointing) of an answer? Anchored by the F word, no less!

He went on to tell me about the pitfalls associated with each of these "buckets." In the start-up world, he was exposed to lots of icky people. When he consulted, there was this issue and that issue. I don't recall many details after absorbing the blow from his initial, one-line response. I just remember thinking, *Well, that dream is done.*

Seriously, in that one conversation, this girl right here who's all about authenticity, who loves to do big, new things, and was running a nine-figure company—who had jumped over INSANE hurdles and had come out on top—was ready to put her dream on the shelf, close the door, and never look back. I even thought, *Good thing I had this conversation with Joe. Otherwise, I can't imagine how bad things would have turned out.*

But—and this is a crucial "but"—I had a coach at that time. Within a week of my call with Joe, my coach and I had our regularly scheduled session. At first, our talk was business as usual. We discussed a challenging employee issue and my plan for an upcoming quarterly business review meeting. With just about ten minutes left in our session, my brain oscillated between whether or not I should also divulge this ***stupid*** idea I had and the feedback Joe had given me on it.

I decided to mention the career thoughts swirling in my head and my conversation with Joe. It would probably be rude to keep her in the dark, and I thought mentioning it quickly would allow me to check this disclosure off my list. I was sure she would quickly place a gold star sticker on my shirt for seeking advice and wisdom from someone else and protecting myself from a career-shattering decision.

But that's not what happened. Instead, she calmly asked me, "What do you think about all that?" The question immediately slowed   me   down.   It's the greatest gift a coach can give you. She allowed me to process what I had heard from Joe. As soon as I started to do that processing work, guess who *finally* showed up to the party? Erin. The real me. The person who had her own thoughts and her own doubts. The person who realized that one person's lemons didn't mean I would end up with a lemon rind in my mouth too.

While that short conversation with my coach solved absolutely nothing, it was just enough to keep me from veering completely off the path to my dream of pursuing something new. It gave me just enough pause to not swing the pendulum 180 degrees back in the other direction. It allowed me to realize that Joe's feedback was input. Nothing more, nothing less. As Bruce Lee once said, "Absorb what is useful. Discard what is not. Add what is uniquely your own."

And God, what I wouldn't have given to have The 50% Rule beating a drum in my head that day. It would have made everything so much easier.

I would have realized that, yes, Joe was right about a few things. Don't go off and work with shitty people. Don't expect to avoid dips and valleys if you decide to become a consultant.

At the same time, I'm not Joe. There are also infinite paths—not just finite buckets—I could choose if I decided to take the leap.

It wasn't until many months later that I even realized that the path I'd eventually choose existed. And I didn't hear about it from a former colleague, mentor, or even my coach. I heard about it on a podcast.

I heard it while—you guessed it, just like we talked about in Chapter 10—collecting random dots and listening to podcasts. This specific podcast was called *Youpreneur*, and I stumbled upon it after about sixteen different twists and turns that led me there. I remember listening to the first episode in my car. I was just a few hundred feet from my house when I heard something that stopped me in my tracks and made me exclaim, out loud, "Wait?! This is exactly what I want to do!" If I had simply listened to what Joe said to me without a single question, I wouldn't have had that epiphany. If I hadn't slowed down, I would have let his words totally eff me up.

Because here's the truth about Joe, and me, and you: Nestled deep in our wisdom, passion to help others, and inability to slow down is our unintended ability to eff people up. And, NEWS FLASH: You do this to people more often than you think.

Nestled deep in our wisdom, passion to help others, and inability to slow down is our unintended ability to eff people up.

In this next section, I want to slow *you* down.

I want to do more than inspire you to pass out The 50% Rule like a business card. I want to ensure you continually give others the space, guidance, and tools to 50% Rule just about everything they do. I want to make you a better leader, mentor, and friend. I want to make you a disciple of The 50% Rule so you can help everyone around you be more authentic and create the ideas/dreams/jobs *they* want to create.

You got that? Now go effing DO it.

14

Share the Cheat Code

I hit my stride. I was 50% Ruling just about everything in sight. And it's not that I wasn't hitting walls. I simply saw them more quickly and then, with increasing ease, deployed my new favorite rule to help me jump over them. When you start using The 50% Rule as your authenticity hack, you will also get over your walls more quickly.

One afternoon, I was working with a coaching client of mine. He had hired me to help him figure out what he wanted to do for his next career move. Once we dug deep to figure that out, we started working together on the right plan of attack to ensure he landed his dream job.

This particular day, we were focused on crafting a killer resume. I talked him through how to create a more authentic summary/opening paragraph, and we dove deep into his superpowers, which would be the foundation for his resume's headline.

We spent over an hour talking it through. I asked him questions and wrote down words I thought were interesting and authentic. I then shared my notes with him and told him to take the notes and incorporate them into a new version of his resume.

But I also had a "gift" for him. I had done a similar exercise with another client, and she had recently shared the incredible feedback she got on her resume. More importantly, this was the resume that helped her land the Senior Director role at the company that was #1 on her target list. She had given me permission to share her blinded resume with other clients of mine to help them create their own authentic resumes.

So, just before we jumped off our call, I asked him if he'd be interested in this sample resume. He said, "Yes." I mean, who doesn't want the playbook that led to near-perfect success for someone else?!

About a week later, in between our coaching calls, he sent me a really long email. He was stuck. He said things like, "Can I say 'I have experience with x, y, z?' I noticed the template doesn't use the word 'Experience.'" Another question was followed by him saying, "I am asking because the third bullet in the resume template states . . ."

That's when Taylor Swift's song hit me like a two-by-four right between my eyes. Was I . . . the problem? I had been strutting my 50% Rule like a perky peacock. Meanwhile, at the same zoo, I was also a lurking crocodile, giving people ideas, examples, and guidance without also handing them The 50% Rule alongside it.

I replied to each of his concerns one by one but reminded him of The Rule: "Remember, always take about half of what you see in that sample and what I tell you, and then do the other 50 percent your own way." He replied right away, telling me how helpful that advice was.

I knew I had just given him the freedom pill to help *him* answer all his questions and create an awesome resume . . . one that was authentically him and not simply fill-in-the-blanks.

• • • • • • • • • • • • •

Templates should be seen less like Waze and more like Walmart greeters. They help point you in the right direction, but you probably shouldn't follow them home.

• • • • • • • • • • • •

Since that day, I have tossed out The 50% Rule in nearly every conversation I've had. And no, it's not like I throw the Slap Ya Mama Cajun spice on things that shouldn't have it. It's just that with almost every barrier people encounter, The 50% Rule is the perfect seasoning to make their lives taste better.

Early in the writing process, I decided I didn't want to do it alone. I wanted to see if a subset of people in the authenticity movement, i.e., on my email list, would be interested in talking to me about their experiences with The 50% Rule.

One of the women who agreed to speak with me is Julie Ann Dubek. At the time of writing this, Julie Ann is the Chief Human Resources Officer for a multi-state health system with over 50,000 employees. Needless to say, Julie Ann has a big, influential job.

When I sent the initial sample chapters out to my quasi-focus group, I included a few paragraphs that roughly outlined what would be in the book. In that outline, I mentioned some ideas about 50% Ruling leadership.

Julie Ann gave her two cents: "This will be so powerful for leaders. In my new gig, I am experiencing people hanging on my every word and randomly expressed thoughts as a 'do this, don't do that.' It's weird and exhausting—and likely frustrating for them too."

It's easy to believe that those "at the top" relish giving advice and having people hang on their every word . . . basking in the glory of having the power to easily get people to think and do things the way *they* think and do them.

But great leaders like Julie Ann recognize their imperfections. They know that their formulas may not work for others, and that they don't always know exactly what to do. Great leaders understand both the power *and* risk of their position.

Julie Ann also sees The 50% Rule as more than a motivator to supercharge her leadership. She sees it as a *relief*—for others and for herself. She sees it as a tangible, more succinct way to express her views. By encouraging The 50% Rule, she doesn't have to worry about creating mini Julie Ann robots wandering around their company's halls.

Oprah Winfrey talked on The goop Podcast about how Maya Angelou once told her, "Babe, you are where you are because you're obedient to the call. And even when I tell you things, I like the way you listen and decide whether it is for you."

Advise, then let them decide. That's how they'll find the real prize.

The 50% Rule may not be as poetic as Maya's words, but it's also a simple way to guide someone to think more like Oprah. Guide them to decide. Guide them to the answer in a way most authentic to them.

And Oprah understood this. She once said, "I had no idea that being your authentic self could make me as rich as I've become. If I had, I'd have done it a lot earlier." Read that one more time.

15

Propel Your Peeps

I desperately want you to get as much as possible from this book. So, to be sure that happens, here's what I want you to do:

1. Read each of the following chapters of this next section in order.
2. After each chapter, pause and make notes on the things that were most impactful for you.
3. One week from completing your notes, review them to ensure you keep everything in mind.
4. Next, implement The 50% Rule with one of your work-related projects.
5. Record what . . .

OMG, I can't even take you all the way through #5. Why? Because a prescribed set of actions likely feels nice on the surface but then quickly morphs inside your soul into a fiery hairball of *I don't want to do this!* Clear? Yes. Motivating? Prolly not.

I talked earlier in the book about the positive impacts of The 50% Rule, including that, when you use it for yourself, it makes it much more fun to do things. But even more important than that is that you can use this rule as a modern-day way to lead others. The 50% Rule will make people significantly more excited and motivated to do the things you need *them* to do so *you* can succeed.

In this chapter, we'll explore the science-y things that make The 50% Rule more than a solution to your Personal Pattern (PP) but rather your ace-in-the-hole to persuade, motivate, and lead others to do great things!

I woke up at 5:45 this morning and drove seventeen minutes to my gym. About four years ago, I joined F45, a franchised gym with over 1,700 studios worldwide. The truth is I've never been a gym lover. My past gym experiences always left me wandering aimlessly, feeling unmotivated, and just doing my best to look cool while I had no clue what I was doing.

But this gym is different; I absolutely love going. I've realized that this is primarily due to their format—a forty-five minute, pre-defined circuit that changes daily. They tell you where to go, what to do, and how long to do it. I've realized that when I work out, I want to be told exactly what actions to take next.

But the gym is the ONLY place in my life where this statement is true.

For everything else in my life, much like my daughter, I know that if I'm told to do something, my motivation takes a nose-dive. If, instead, I have some hand in coming up with the idea/task/to-do, then get the frick out of the way, I will get it done. And your head will spin watching me do it.

So, the big question is: Are most people like me? That is, are people generally more motivated when the idea/task/to-do is, at least in part, their own idea? Or is this just another Erin PP?

In 1977, a few other dudes had this question too. Psychologists Edward L. Deci and Richard M. Ryan met while they were both at the University of Rochester. To say they dug into this question would be an understatement.

Neither Deci nor Ryan bought into the conventional motivational wisdom, i.e., that money is people's biggest motivator. So, they set out on years of experiments and research that eventually fed into what is known as Self-Determination Theory. Although they performed many experiments over the years, one experiment in particular fascinated me the most.

In 1978, Deci and others published the results of a study funded by a grant from the National Institute of Mental Health. In this experiment, they brought in control groups and participant groups (you know, typical research-y stuff) to work on complex, 3-D puzzles. One group was called the "task choice" group, and the other was the "no-choice" group. Let's just call them Choice Group and No Choice Group.

Choice Group was shown six diagrams of puzzles and they were told they could choose three of them to work on (50 percent! It's everywhere, my friend!). This group was also told they could choose the amount of time, within the full thirty minutes, they would work on the three puzzles they chose. No Choice Group was instead given the three puzzles they *had* to work on and how much time they had to work on each.

Now, in a plot twist that I feel like every smarty-pants researcher pulls, but for some reason nobody sees coming, they didn't actually care about the groups' puzzle-solving abilities, i.e., the time it took for Choice Group vs. No Choice Group to solve their puzzles. Instead, once they completed the thirty-minute puzzle-solving stint, they moved on to what they were *really* after.

The observer made up an excuse about why they needed to leave the room for ten-ish minutes. Since both groups had finished their puzzles, each group had the same remaining items in their rooms—three puzzles and three magazines, the latter of which were strategically placed in the rooms as well. The observer told both groups that they could do whatever they wanted while they waited for their return. Hint: This was the *real* part of the experiment.

While the observer was doing their fake work, another person was observing the two rooms to calculate how much time each group *continued* to spend working on puzzles, as opposed to reading magazines or shooting the shit (of course, no one had a smartphone in the seventies, so scrolling social media wasn't an option).

They found that, on average, Choice Groupers worked on the puzzles over 50 percent more than the No Choice Groupers. This proved that choice, or autonomy, in completing a task was a *major* factor in motivating people, not just initially, but on an ongoing basis. This experiment led to the creation of one of the three basic tenets of the Self-Determination Theory. This theory suggests that people are motivated by three primary things:

1. **Autonomy:** The freedom to have a say in what they're doing.
2. **Competence:** The need to do something they have experience in doing.
3. **Relatedness:** The need to feel connected to what they're doing.

These are monumental findings. Sit in this for a moment. Not just in the words on the page but also in what is *not* on the page. People are NOT motivated by:

1. Logic
2. Force
3. Money

Instead, I want you to consider The 50% Rule as the kindling to your new leadership fire. Start handing out The 50% Rule as your number-one motivation fire starter. Wear a 50% Rule badge wherever you go. The 50% Rule hands your team the gift of autonomy mixed with competence mixed with relatedness on a flammable silver platter.

Wear a 50% Rule badge wherever you go.

When I work with my business coaching clients—CEOs/presidents of small to mid-sized companies—I say "50% Rule It" at least once every time we talk. In fact, many of my clients now preempt me and tell me things like "I should probably 50% Rule that" before I can even get the words out.

When discussing a new project with a team member, outline what you need or know. But then explain The 50% Rule to them in your own way.

If you're mentoring someone, after you tell them about a great lesson you learned or a path you took, remind them only to take about half of what they hear from you and then let the other half of their journey be their own.

When presenting in front of a large audience, place The 50% Rule right at the beginning to let them know to listen to you for the inspiration that sticks and to toss aside the stuff that doesn't land for them.

When you have a new project teed up, and you're meeting with your employees to have them take the lead, outline what you *think* is critical to the project's success, but then gift them The 50% Rule to give them the autonomy they need to do the work because they *want* to, not because they *have* to.

When your kid asks you for help on an essay they're writing, give them your thoughts but then tell them they're simply thought-starters and that they should 50% Rule what you told them.

Or best yet, buy this book for everyone you know. ;-)

Lead with 50, motivate 100.

REAL PEEPS STORY

A PERPLEXING PEOPLE PUZZLE

The pandemic was over(ish), and corporate leaders everywhere were thrown into a new crisis—how to handle their return-to-office policy. For Julie Ann Dubek, the Chief Human Resources Officer for a multi-state health system with over 50,000 employees, this was a complex equation she'd never had to solve before. Compounding Julie Ann's company's equation was the fact that they employed thousands of employees in bedside roles, so remote work wasn't an option for many of their employees.

As Julie Ann and her team started gathering data and input to help form their policy, she recalls the overwhelm they felt. "EVERYBODY has an opinion about work arrangements and locations. Countless external business journal articles and leader opinions had been shared, and the recommendations ranged from CEOs demanding everyone return to the office to businesses closing corporate offices and exclusively employing remote workers. We also had plenty of input from team members, executives, and board members on what we 'should' do."

She and her team trudged through the input and recommendations, and she also conducted her own research in partnership with Arizona State University. At the same time, Julie Ann was also several months into being part of The 50% Rule collaboration team, and she had become a big believer in using The Rule in many aspects of her life.

After compiling their research and input, The 50% Rule helped her realize that it was okay to not be binary in their decision, i.e., one policy for all. Julie Ann said, "Our team recognized that a 'one size fits all' approach (i.e., all corporate employees must work from the office or all work remotely) was not a logical solution, leading us to utilize The 50% Rule. By utilizing best practices for remote and in-office work arrangements, we were able to instead focus less on policy and more on unique needs."

For example, they decided to allow leaders the freedom to determine whether their organization would be most successful with in-office, remote, or hybrid workers. Her HR team focused on providing education and toolkits for those who planned to participate in a flexible work arrangement. They also established an automated annual attestation process to document the success and opportunities of every hybrid or remote work arrangement, as well as metrics to assess things such as engagement, retention, and productivity.

But they didn't stop there. They knew they had to also focus on the *other* 50 percent of the equation: making working IN the office more collaborative and fun. To do that, they created updated office "bullpen" areas for collaboration, added more vibrant decor and colors, established a lounge area with games, a pool table, TVs, etc., and encouraged the use of an on-site gym and cafe. They even offered acupuncture services.

Julie Ann talks about the positives that came out of 50% Ruling their return-to-office strategy. "After all we put in place, we have seen a number of benefits. We had a 4 percent increase in positive responses to both 'employee engagement' and 'sense of belonging' on our annual employee survey, we have more opportunities to recruit diverse populations from more locations, and we are demonstrating a culture of trust and innovation."

After Julie Ann had success using The 50% Rule to shape their return-to-office plan, she asked me to help her talk about The Rule and its power to her direct leadership team, as well as approximately eighty leaders participating in their leadership development program. Julie Ann provided her take on The 50% Rule to the teams, saying "I'm a rule follower by nature. I wish I had known about *this* rule thirty years ago."

SECTION 4:

. . . .

50% YOUR BUSINESS GROWTH

16

Awww, The 50% Rule is Growing Up

By now, I hope you're feeling inspired and energized to use The 50% Rule to go out and make some waves, for yourself and the people around you. But look, at the end of the day, I'm not a motivational speaker. I'm a get-business-done-better speaker.

I'm a businesswoman at heart. Although I'd LOVE to help you crush your career, reach your dreams, and feel a hell of a lot better doing it, I also want you to get big stuff accomplished. As a former corporate CEO who used authenticity as her #1 strategy for success, I would never have raised the Success Flag if I felt like a rock star but our business results were in the pooper.

Until now, we've primarily focused on Sleeprunning Syndrome and how activating The 50% Rule can give you immunity to the symptoms it causes. We've talked about how The 50% Rule can help you as an individual to propel your career, be a better leader, chase your dreams, etc.

But there is another syndrome that festers and builds within a bunch of Sleeprunners scurrying around a company: **Sameness Syndrome**. Sameness Syndrome is the institutional version of Sleeprunning Syndrome. It happens when a company's Sleeprunners focus more on doing what feels normal instead of what feels needed. Here are some of the symptoms of a business suffering from Sameness Syndrome:

- Its strategy throws everything at the wall instead of standing for one unique thing (and against some others).

- The company messaging sounds noble and perfect, but there is no human voice or explanation of what the business actually *does*.

- The business focuses on "innovation" that has to be delivered via million-dollar IT projects documents.

Your mission, products, and messaging travel on a non-stop conveyor belt that passes through the hands of the company's coterie of consultants, overlords, and VPs. By the time everything comes out the other side of the factory, you have a pristine product and message, but they're EXACTLY THE SAME AS YOUR COMPETITORS'. (And then you want to throw up when you lose another client to one of your same-y competitors that's doing the exact same thing as you are.)

In this next section, we will step things up a notch and give you a cure for Sameness Syndrome. We'll take those 50% Rule big-kid pants and put The Rule in a full-fledged Gucci suit, so you can use the fundamental principles to innovate your business without sprinting, scrumming, or spending millions of dollars.

I want to give you the courage and inspiration to step forward with The 50% Rule in a way that goes well beyond your personal growth and the growth of others. I'll share stories of innovations and successes that came from people using The 50% Rule to catapult their businesses. My goal is to create a canvas and space that helps you color in your own ideas and dream of ways in which you can do big things in your business too.

You don't have to be Elon Musk or Jeff Bezos to do big things. Your business' innovation doesn't have to come from AI or fancy systems or your willingness to sacrifice everything. It can come from recognizing the underlying patterns that launched others' successes and then applying those patterns to your product, department, or company.

Finally, most 50% Rule ideas grow out of three simple ingredients: playful thought, passion, and persistence. But I know you might be running a massive company or at least leading a complex business unit, and you can't necessarily innovate simply by throwing out The 50% Rule to your teams like swag bags at a conference. You have meetings and structure and lawyers. You need a system or a set of guideposts and prompts to help you scale The Rule. That's why I've also included a chapter that gives you The 50% Rule (I)nnovation Framework, which will help you more formally enact The Rule if you work in a big behemoth of a company.

17

Don't Give Away Your Shot

Eleven Tony Awards.

Pulitzer Prize for Drama.

Grammy Award for Best Musical Theater Album.

Twenty-plus other awards.

Over one billion dollars grossed.

And most importantly—because she's my authentic North Star—Michelle Obama referred to it as "the best piece of art in any form I have ever seen in my life."

Yes, this is the story of The 50% Rule G.O.A.T., *Hamilton*.

It was the summer of 2008, and Lin-Manuel Miranda and his then-girlfriend, now-wife, left the busy chaos of New York for a much-needed vacation in Mexico. While there, Miranda decided this trip was the perfect time to crack open a book, and he landed on reading the *New York Times* bestselling book by Ron Chernow, *Alexander Hamilton*. Only a few chapters in, he imagined telling this story. On Broadway. Through hip-hop music. Say what?!

When he returned home, he contacted an unlikely potential collaborator, Jeremy McCarter. About ten years earlier, McCarter was a drama critic who wrote an article about how Broadway was missing a huge opportunity to infuse hip-hop music into its repertoire. Miranda and McCarter had bonded just months earlier over this shared vision, and Miranda couldn't wait to tell him about his cockamamie idea to moonwalk hip-hop all the way back to 1776.

While you might think that Miranda's mega Broadway hit, *Hamilton*, was the first time he or others infused hip-hop and rap into the more traditional Broadway genre, that isn't the case. Miranda also did this with the first show he created, *In the Heights*.

But it wasn't until that day in Mexico, while reading the story of this lesser-known Founding Father, that Miranda ignited The 50% Rule.

Miranda realized that Hamilton's legacy was his words' impact on the United States. An author of the Constitution and the most significant contributor to the creation of the Federalist Papers, Hamilton had moved the U.S. forward through the power of his words. Miranda believed hip-hop packed a word punch that would greatly surpass the splash of any breathtaking Broadway ballad.

Much like he had believed with *In the Heights*, Miranda thought that telling Hamilton's story through hip-hop would be, using today's hip term, meta. Beyond that, while most had assumed Hamilton was a Mayflower American, Miranda instead saw the Founding Father as an immigrant from an island about 120 miles from Miranda's own family's place of origin. Hamilton's unique profile bolstered Miranda's belief that this show called for a unique musical twist.

There's a reason why you may have never heard of *In the Heights* but get all giddy and teary-eyed when I simply mention the name "Hamilton." (BEST. BROADWAY. SHOW. EVER.) A story like *In the Heights*, which is primarily about contemporary people in New York City, has a plausible setting for hip-hop music.

But a story about a bunch of white dudes who wore wigs and wrote with feather pens over 200 years ago? Well, hearing that told mostly through a non-white cast singing hip-hop is about the least expected thing you can imagine. You see, juxtapositions create joyful jolts. Miranda's *Hamilton* wasn't even the first Broadway show about Alexander Hamilton. Mary Hamlin wrote and brought to life a play by the same name in 1917. Despite good reviews, it only ran about eighty shows. I'm guessing that she did NOT 50% Rule her show.

Juxtapositions create joyful jolts.

I talked about the Six Principles of Strategic Authenticity (H.U.M.A.N.S.) in my first book (the H stands for *humility*; U for *unexpected*; M for *model*, as in "show, don't tell"; A for *adapt*; N for *narrate*; and S for *spark*). Yes, I know "strategic authenticity" sounds all kinds of icky, but the reality is that authenticity isn't simply about being yourself. That fluffy unicorn doo-doo may sound fanciful for a hot second until you realize that if everyone walked around like they were in an airport where no one was looking, we'd have a workplace and world filled with Cheetos-eating, nose-picking, flatulence-airing people. *That's* actually being faux-thentic. No frickin' thanks.

The word authenticity originates from the Greek word *authentikos*. It means to be genuine, original, and authoritative. Being original (or "unexpected") is critical to being authentic and reaping the mega rewards that are scientifically linked to authenticity. Without focusing on being unexpected and creating curiosity, people will ignore you like you ignore your child's PTA newsletter.

They'll tune out. They'll pass you by. They won't see you EVEN IF YOU'RE GREAT. You'll be ignored if you're doing something great but expected. "Unexpected" wakes people up. Unexpected gets noticed. Something unexpected that is *also* great, like *Hamilton*? Well, that gets you more than noticed. UNEXPECTED + GREAT gets you fame, awards, and loads of money (if you're into that kind of thing!).

Be "great" and people will still be bored. Be "great" *and* "unexpected" and people will be floored.

Putting together two seemingly contradictory things is one of the best ways to innovate your business and catapult your success. Patrice Banks, founder of Girls Auto Clinic and the sheCANic® brand, is another exemplar of the power of juxtapositions.

When Patrice became increasingly frustrated that she and many other women weren't encouraged or empowered to learn how to take care of their cars on their own, she decided to do something about it. While still working as an engineer at DuPont, she decided to go back to school: automotive technology school. Once she completed the program, she made the seemingly ludicrous decision to trade in her six-figure job to make $600 per week so she could get her hands dirty (literally) and learn what it would take to run an auto shop. In 2017, she opened Girls Auto Clinic in Darby, Pennsylvania, a repair shop with an all-female staff of mechanics.

Amazing, right? It's certainly unexpected and unique for her to open an all-female repair shop. However, it was when Banks decided to 50% Rule her shop and mash together two unique things that everything exploded. She realized that although women loved her shop's approach, it was still hard for them give up their precious time to bring their cars. To help women kill two birds with one stone, she grabbed the space next door to the shop and created Clutch Lounge and Beauty Bar, where women can get everything from a hair blowout to a pedicure while waiting for their car to be fixed.

Banks's 50% Ruled shop has gotten attention from *Good Morning America*, NPR's *Fresh Air*, and *People* magazine. In fact, Patrice is even working with a producer at Warner Bros on a potential scripted comedy about Girls Auto Clinic!

For Banks, the mashing of juxtaposed worlds was intentional and meant to solve a real world issue. With Girls Auto Clinic, Banks put women + auto repair together so she could better serve her customers. Other times, the mash-up can simply derive from loving two opposing worlds and having the guts to put them together.

With Hamilton, Miranda didn't marry hip-hop with Broadway because he needed to solve a problem. He married them together because he loved them both, and he saw how these two opposing styles could bring out the best in each other.

And if you think I gave *Hamilton* the 50% Rule G.O.A.T. trophy simply because it got tons of accolades, made loads of money, and I went to see it twice in one week, you'd only be half-right. What I love most about Miranda's 50% Ruling magnificence is that he kept 50%ing the show, well beyond the musical composition.

The 50% Rule can also be found in the actors' costumes. Miranda and his team decided to forego period wigs and hair and instead have the actors go modern from the neck up, eighteenth century from the neck down. He also made the decision to 50% Rule the music. Miranda artfully combines hip-hop with classical Broadway ballads throughout the show. This allows you to experience the thrill of consuming something fresh and new while also enjoying some of the classic Broadway anthems that have likely filled your cup so many other times.

Also, while *Hamilton* primarily follows the traditional Broadway musical format, it includes zero dialogue. Classic Broadway shows toggle between music and dialogue to tell the whole story. Miranda found that with the rapid pace of hip-hop music, adding dialogue felt like too much of a contrast and deceleration to the show's energy. So he left it out. 50% Rule mic drop.

To bring this down from what feels like untouchable artistry to real-person reality, here's an example of what went through my head as soon as I took a break from writing this chapter.

As I prepared to release this book, our launch strategy was constantly on my mind. What you might not know about authors is that although writing the actual book is a bit of a Herculean effort, marketing the book is WAY harder. And for most, a more dreaded task. Me included.

As I thought about doing the book launch for this puppy, I immediately felt the onset of many of the Sleeprunning Syndrome symptoms. I first got a stitch in my side, feeling those damn Comparison Cramps coming on. I thought, *I can't possibly be as successful in launching this book as this person and that person. Their following is much bigger on social media, blah, blah.*

It quickly spread and manifested itself into Self-Doubt Gout. For me, that gout didn't fester around my talent—it was about my stick-to-it-iveness. I know I'm a great starter but a not-so-great finisher. I ruminated, *I'll start out great, but I'll quickly lose energy and steam.*

Ultimately, what just about put me on bed rest was the Finish Fatigue I felt when I thought about having to complete a 20-page project plan filled with all the tasks I'd need to execute for a great book launch playbook.

In the words of Roy Kent from *Ted Lasso*, I screamed inside, *Fuuuuuuuuuuuuuudge.*

And no, this is not an exaggeration. Despite writing a book I was so excited for people to read, thinking about launching this bad boy made me feel all these ailments and more.

Until.

I remembered the gosh darn 50% Rule that I *should* have been using. After I wrote the first draft of this chapter, I went upstairs to the shower, the place where most of my best 50% Rule ideas are born.

As I thought about the very words and lessons I just preached to you, I started thinking about the book launch. I thought: *What are the things* I *love that* I *might be able to marry with my book launch?* My brain started firing out these things:

- Sports

- Tailgating

- Beer

- Yard games

- Non-fancy shit

Before I could get any further on my list, I immediately envisioned a book tour like no other. I thought, *What if instead of a stuffy road show, bouncing between snoozy bookstores and boring coffee shops, I did a tailgate book tour?!*

I could pick a few venues—a football game, an outdoor concert, maybe even a few readers' front yards. We could forego people lining up in a painfully long, boring line just to get thirty seconds with me to sign their book. Or Gawwwd, even worse, we could ditch me awkwardly reading chapters from the book like it was my daughter's birthday and I was her class's mystery reader.

Instead, what if we gathered some folks to sit in lawn chairs, throw some cornhole, and tip back some IPAs, while others would be welcome to stop by our folding table with *The 50% Rule* there for anyone who needs a little kick in the rear? I went from bedridden to pumped in 2.2 seconds! Doing a Tailgate Tour sounded like a helluva lot more fun to me. Not to mention, I'm pretty sure it would probably check the unexpected box and grab the attention of others attending the game or event.

50% Rule innovation is like setting up your two best friends on a blind date and giving them permission to make whoopee.

If you look, you'll see this unexpected 50% Rule marriage present in many successful shows in the last few decades, on stage and on screen. *The Office* marries traditional sitcom writing with documentary-style camera shots and dialogue. *The Simpsons* created a billion-dollar-plus empire by combining cartoons, previously a medium used only for children, with adult satire and humor. *South Park* took that to the next level by mixing cartoons with massively barnyard language and often controversial, contemporary, and politically incorrect topics.

As you think about your business, what are two things that you love? And not just *business* things you love, but overall products, experiences, events, and passions. What product or process do you offer that is expected . . . a commodity? What is something completely unrelated but that you love how it's done? What would it look like if you married the expected and the unexpected together?

As John Kander, a famous Broadway composer, once said while talking about *Hamilton*: "Innovators are usually synthesizers—they synthesize everything they know and add their own personal talents, and out comes something new." Or, said another way by synthesizing a line from my favorite *Hamilton* song, "My Shot":

It's time for YOU to pop a squat on conventional wisdom.

REAL PEEPS STORY
·······························

A TOUGH SELL

Cori Rolland and her colleague had a creative, powerful, and semi-sassy business idea. That's the good news. The bad news is they needed to pitch it inside their company, which operates in a largely traditional, highly regulated industry.

When Cori's company announced a "challenge" to develop an innovative healthcare program, she was excited. It was the perfect opportunity to use The 50% Rule. She and her colleague saw a major gap in the healthcare industry related to two very common, yet often undiscussed, female conditions: endometriosis and polycystic ovary syndrome (PCOS.)

You're not alone if you don't know what these are. Here's a little background. Women with PCOS don't ovulate regularly or sometimes at all, which creates infertility issues. It's also sometimes linked to weight gain and other conditions. It's thought to be caused by a metabolic and hormonal imbalance, and one in every five women has the condition. I didn't know what PCOS was until I heard Cori's story.

I also didn't know what endometriosis was until I was diagnosed with it sixteen years ago. Every month, when women ovulate, they release tissue to create a little "woobie blanket" inside their uterus in case they need to harbor any fugitives . . . I mean, babies. Women with endometriosis release a similar tissue outside their uterus, where it cozies up to other organs. The tissue is basically lost as hell and can't get out. It's painful and also causes infertility. Your body is like, Ehhh, you're doing it wrong. No baby for you.

Despite being common, on average, these conditions take seven to ten years to diagnose. Insanity. That was certainly the case for me; I wasn't diagnosed with endometriosis until about twenty years after I first menstruated and a few years into (unsuccessfully) trying to get pregnant. That's a big problem.

Cori and her team recognized the root cause of the issue. Although these were common conditions, they were plagued by the fact that talking about anything roughly related to a woman's period is often seen as taboo. They believed that better consumer awareness was key. If women could align their pain and challenges with these less-than-talked-about conditions, they could significantly reduce the time it took to diagnose and treat them.

However, to do this, they needed to ditch conventional medical speak. That info was already ALL over the interweb, but it wasn't effective. Instead, they needed to do something edgier . . . more unexpected. Cori says of their unique opportunity, "We needed to find a way to design the program and marketing that met conservative brand guidelines but with a fresh design and voice outside of what the company normally would have accepted."

They were targeting a younger population and wanted to find a more modern way to appeal to them. This would be a challenging internal sell, though. They were working in a

160+-year-old healthcare company that employed tons of overlords who were conditioned to keep things on the straight and narrow.

Here's Cori: "I knew if we approached it in the traditional corporate way, we wouldn't appeal to that audience. But I also knew that if we took it too far, it wouldn't get internal approval. We had to find a way to do both. The 50% Rule was our guide to achieving both.

We outlined the usual marketing channels that the company would approve. In that way, we stayed within the corporate box. That was the traditional 50%. But the content, style, and message within those channels . . . we tipped that box on its side."

Her program partner was an incredible graphic designer who was just as passionate about getting the message across in a way no one had seen before.

One of the new 50 percent approaches was creating an interactive website called LittleRedLies.com. Cori said, "We knew this conversation was uncomfortable for women (which is why it takes seven to ten years to get diagnosed), so we made it okay to be uncomfortable and then gave them tools to have the conversation with their family and doctor."

They didn't blanket the site with information and statistics. Instead, they made it fun, interactive, and authentic. For example, instead of asking women for information about their period and giving them normal response options (e.g., "heavy, medium, or light"), they gave them options like "White pants are okay with me." The site also features a creative video, kicked off by women taking a fun, true THE

50% RULE quiz on common period-related facts and myths. And then those same women get serious and talk about the years of misinformation, misdiagnosis, pain, and shame they experienced.

They also 50% Ruled the marketing, but it took some give and take. When they first suggested a more catchy and unique in-store strategy using bold signage, Cori and her team were told they couldn't do that. Resolved not to do "traditional" marketing, Cori said her team would pull in-store marketing from their plan. That tough stance catalyzed the marketing team to come back to them and compromise. Cori says, "They came back with 50 percent of what we wanted, and I compromised on the other 50 percent."

They then marched forward, replacing the traditional, informative-yet-static signs with ones that had a proactive question. For example, they hung bouncy signs in the CVS Health feminine products aisle that said, "It's just those pesky hormones. Or is it? LittleRedLies.com." Cori says, "We were able to meet brand guidelines by giving a little but getting brand marketing to give a little too. We went in with conviction on our 50 percent approach. We didn't say: Can we do this? We said: Why can't we do this?"

When I asked Cori about the benefits of The 50% Rule, she said it made the team realize there was a path to shake things up. But to do that, they needed to meet halfway. She said, "I learned how to take things we knew we needed to do differently and wrap it around the 50 percent the corporation would be willing to swallow. It really helped us position our ideas to be accepted. In the end, they even trademarked Little Red Lies™!"

After the launch, they received a tremendous amount of positive feedback. People said things like, "This is me, my sister, my daughter, my best friend, my wife." They received emails of support from colleagues, friends, and family. One email said it best: "I finally feel heard." And Cori felt energized by their results. She said, "It was my proudest moment at that company."

Check out their site, LittleRedLies.com. And if you're working on something new and feeling a cramp, feel free to 50% Rule this story to get you back into your creative flow.

18

Two Rights Make it Righter

Wouldn't it have been great to have been born in, like, the early twentieth century?

I mean, yes, there were depressions, no smartphones, and life was basically terrible for anyone who wasn't a rich white man. But there was also so much room for innovation. So many things hadn't yet been thought of. It was innovation heaven!

And now, when you're pressed to think more innovatively, doesn't it feel like all the good ideas are taken, or at least like you have to be a rocket scientist to innovate?

You sit down to innovate a new product or service at your company and, voila, your competitor already offers it. You dream of starting a side gig, but it feels like everyone's miles ahead of you. You have a business idea, but after five minutes of Googling, you realize your idea is already taken. By a thousand people.

That's how it must feel if you're an aspiring contestant on *America's Got Talent (AGT)*. Now in its gazillionth season, surely we've seen every animated dance troupe and flame-throwing married couple out there. I can't imagine how many more magicians can somehow know what the last soft drink Howie consumed was and make it magically appear inside a yellow balloon.

Possibly the least innovative category to take the stage on this show is singing. Sure, we all love to hear a good soprano climax that vibrates the room and our soul. But it also can get all been-there-seen-that. And "seen-that" doesn't win million-dollar competitions.

That's why when Merissa Beddows took the stage during the 2022 season of *AGT*, I went from half watching while multi-tasking-on-my-phone mode to can't-look-away mode. Merissa began her audition by singing a traditional opera song. At first I had the same reaction as Simon Cowell: *Whatevs, sounds amazing but seen-that.*

But then she did something completely unexpected and whipped out a large die. On that die, she had the names of several people, and she asked the judges to roll the die every so often while she was singing. Each time they rolled a new name, she would continue singing opera BUT do it in that person's voice.

She sang opera in the voices of Ariana Grande, Snow White, and her grandmother. She even did an opera song in Siri's voice. Yes, your personal iPhone assistant Siri. It was beautiful and powerful and hilarious, all at the same time.

After her audition, I picked up my phone, not to multitask again but to immediately document her performance in my 50% Rule notes. What Merissa did was genius. She didn't do anything new; instead, she combined two great but opposing talents—opera singing and impressionism. She finished to a standing ovation and placed in the top 10 overall!

So often, it's easy to feel like innovating and standing out has to be doing something *totally* new . . . that innovation has to be new technology or an entirely new way of doing things. Instead, innovation often comes simply by taking 50 percent of one normal thing and doing it with 50 percent of another totally normal thing.

As you think about your next big idea, what are two things you love and can bring together? As you prepare to innovate, simply write down a list of experiences, products, workflows, etc., that you've had a great experience with. Take stock of things WAY outside your industry.

What have others done well? What experiences do you often tell others about? What recent technology features do you see as a trend? What has the crazy world of AI technology made so much easier than before?

Here are some random examples to show you how this strategy can work, well beyond innovating music:

- You recently traveled, and the hotel asked you what your favorite snacks were when you booked it and then had them waiting for you in your room. A week later at work, you're tasked with creating a process for onboarding new customers to your technology platform. You know that the technology setup will take about an hour for the customer to complete. You decide to create a process that sends your new customers a twenty-dollar coupon to DoorDash to get lunch to eat while they complete the approximate one-hour setup. Hotel customization + food delivery = a technology onboarding process that nobody has ever seen before!

Result: Your customers can't stop telling others about your product, all simply because you merged two beloved categories—food and technology—making two rights "righter."

- You're interviewing for a marketing job where you know you're the underdog. You recently saw an online ad campaign that simply displayed a QR code that took you to an uplifting, funny TikTok video. You also secretly watch the show *Let's Make a Deal* anytime you're looking for some mind-numbing relief. Rather than going into the interview with your standard resume and rehearsed answers to those cringy behavioral questions, you decide to bring in just one piece of paper with three QR codes on it, with Door #1, Door #2, and Door #3 written next to each. When the interviewer is intrigued and can't resist whipping out their phone to scan one of the three "doors," they're taken to one of three TikTok videos with you dancing and text that bullets some details about one of your top three qualities, e.g., communication, creativity, and collaboration.

  Result: Because you combined two not-so-new things and delivered them in a totally new environment, you created an unforgettable interview experience. Not to mention, it's for a *marketing* job—so you demonstrated your marketing genius. They offer you the job before you walk out the door.

- You want to become a coach, but it feels like there are a bazillion of them out there. Oh, and they're all miles ahead of you. You're a businesswoman, and so you naturally gravitate towards the executive coaching "box." However, your true passion lies in the areas of health and nutrition. But becoming a nutritionist just ain't gonna pay the bills (or stimulate that businesswoman inside of you). As you stop to think about what has worked for you and your career, you realize that a big part of your career success hasn't just been tied to work-related things. Nutrition has been a game-changer for you, and when done well, it has significantly impacted your health *and* your career. You decide to create an entirely new category of coaching by combining two well-established coaching professions— executive coaching and health coaching.

Result: You create unique demand for your coaching services since you're in a category all your own. Note: This is a true story about one of my coaching clients and the path we co-created and that she's now pursuing full bore!

These examples didn't come from spending a boatload of money on new technology. They aren't born from a 112-page PowerPoint delivered by a $5 million McKinsey project. They aren't based on months of research and committees. Instead, they came to me based on giving myself about fifteen minutes of quiet space to let my head dream and wander and recall those little things in life that light me, and others, up.

If you think about it, *most* innovations aren't entirely new but rather two things coming together. In fact, there's a name for this kind of innovation in the patent world. They're called "Combination Inventions." Some examples include:

- Cronuts: In 2013, Dominique Ansel, a French baker, combined two utterly luscious pastries—a croissant and a donut.

- Skateboard suitcases: Have you seen these things? A classic example of "Crap, why didn't I think of this?!" There are now kids' suitcases that roll around the airport on a flip-down skateboard.

- Dyson vacuum: James Dyson created a vacuum that swivels around, which is the result of combining a traditional vacuum with an invention he came up with thirty years earlier when he made a wheelbarrow with a ball instead of a wheel.

- Dominos: Dominos seized the emerging self-driving car technology (in 2017!) and merged it with pizza delivery.

- Picture-taking drones: Developed by professors from the University of Pennsylvania, they merged drone technology with cameras that are now used for everything from filming sporting events to tracking down criminals.

Conventional innovation wisdom says to start with the customer's needs first and then build your innovation from there. But as Henry Ford said, if he had asked people what they needed, he would have had to try to invent faster horses. Many times, people have NO clue what's possible.

Instead, I would argue that you should look more often at finding two right things to combine.

What are some recent innovations in technology, manufacturing, food, beauty, or whatever other industries you pay attention to? How can you take a piece from those new innovations and combine them with something in your industry?

Your clients may not know they'd love lunch while implementing your software. Your fans may have no clue how AI can help you create a unique experience for them. Your customers may not even think they want a chocolate chip cookie driven by a self-driving car to their doorstep at three p.m., their chocolate-craving witching hour.

Most importantly, executing ideas like these doesn't take grit; it takes guts. It takes cojones to speak up and show people that taking 50 percent of one simple thing + 50 percent of another simple thing IS innovation. Doing something that doesn't necessarily need a 14-page project plan or a $10 million IT project can actually be the very thing that makes your business stand out and succeed.

Implementing 50% Rule innovation doesn't take grit; it takes guts.

And, in case you missed the most important thing I said in this chapter, I'll repeat it: **You and your team need space to innovate.**

Quiet space.

Space not attached to Slack.

Space not sitting at desks.

Space not attached to meetings and to-dos.

Space to get lost.

Space to take wrong turns.

Space to experiment.

Space to feel uncomfortable.

Space to dream.

Space to find the rights, combine the rights, and make things righter.

Now, go wander.

19
Take Me Out of the Ballgame

Seventh-inning stretch

We've spent about "seven innings" together now, and there's a chance you're thinking something like, *This is an interesting concept and book, but isn't The 50% Rule just a synonym for innovation?*

I get it. You've probably been on a journey with this book that first had you drinking the Kool-Aid. But then, at one point, you took a break from reading, and when you came back, you might have looked at that Kool-Aid and seen your glass was half-empty.

I want us to collectively take a quick break, stand up, stretch, and then talk briefly about this baby elephant in the room that might be sucking up your Kool-Aid. Because I would never ever want you to think I'm some mindset archaeologist who found the first-ever tailbone from a T-Rex, only to then have you realize that a million others have found them too. They're just called coccyx bones.

I recognize that The 50% Rule isn't something new, absolute, or even totally real. Its lines are fuzzy, and sometimes it creeps close to feeling like good old-fashioned concepts like innovation, creativity, rebellion, or the word I *almost* love more than my children: authenticity.

In fact, The 50% Rule is ALL those things. As mentioned earlier in the book, this rule was my secret weapon for years to help propel my authenticity forward. As I've learned, mainly through the process of writing this book, The 50% Rule is also a speed pass for innovation, creativity, and continual rebellion against the status quo when the status quo just isn't cutting it.

If you've started to overanalyze and question whether or not this book is teaching you anything new, I want to settle that right now—it's not. My goal isn't to "invent" something new but to hit you over the head with so many examples and stories of something I've called The 50% Rule for the last four years.

My hope is that this ridiculously simple mantra will propel you to stop competing with others and start creating an entirely new path. I want you to realize that your days of feeling like you have to keep up with everyone are over. OVER! Instead, you can have great success while also feeling a helluva lot more confident by finding ways to compete with no one.

And look, if you did start to poo-poo in the Kool-Kool, I get it. But I would also challenge you. If you're thinking, *I already 50% Rule everything*, then why do you still feel so many Sleeprunning Syndrome symptoms? Why do you keep getting Copying Calluses from doing stuff you don't want to do, just to be sure you check the boxes others are checking? Why haven't you started that new business you've always dreamed of doing? Do you get all hyped-up but inevitably end up in bed, suffering from Perfection

Pain? Do you struggle to grow your business, even though you and your team work your buttskis off? Do you want to pull your hair out when your work rivals get promoted while you keep getting the gift of the next big "stretch" assignment?

Or, if you're like me, do you keep doing stupid shit in your personal life, like being ping-ponged between your chiropractor and physical therapist, who keep telling you the other person is wrong. Then it takes you six months to realize you need to 50% Rule those two as well (more on that in Chapter 24), even though you WROTE A DAMN BOOK ON THE 50% RULE?!

Whenever I explain The 50% Rule to someone new, they respond with something like, "Oh yeah, that's so important. I do that with X or Y or Z."

While I love that they immediately support the concept, I also know that they, and probably you, do it in some parts of their lives but miss the memo elsewhere.

You have more Sleeprunning Syndrome ailments than you realize. More importantly, most of those ailments can be cured if you break out The 50% Rule more quickly and more often than you do today. In fact, I'm certain about this. Because I'm writing a book on it, and I still get SS from time to time.

That's why I named it. That's why I preach it. That's why I'm torturing you with an entire book on it. Even if some of it feels hokey, once you've finished this book, it'll be so ridiculously ingrained in you that when the SS symptoms pop up ('cause they always will; you can't avoid them), you'll get healthy and thrive exponentially faster.

This book is no different than the conditioning a professional athlete does. Sure, everyone can kick a ball or throw a baseball, but those who practice, do the work, and repeat it until they want to hurl are so much better than those who click "like" on an inspirational quote by Babe Ruth every so often and then wonder why they're picked last for the team.

I want to be sure you're picked first. You with me? If so, it's time to head back to the game. Let's play ball!

It was the seventh inning, and as he looked up into the stands, The 50% Rule smacked him across the face. But not in a good way.

For Jesse Cole, his journey to riding The 50% Rule up and over the rainbow started in a thunderstorm. Cole took over the baseball program at the historic (and historically unsuccessful) Grayson Stadium in Savannah, Georgia, in 2016. Just a few years later, he was filling the stadium.

He and his team had done a gazillion things to revitalize Grayson's collegiate Summer League baseball team, including crowdsourcing a new, super-duper catchy name: the Savannah Bananas. The Bananas didn't just play baseball; they infused traditional games with entertainment through mid-game TikTok dance routines and a "dad bod cheerleading squad." Directionally, things were going great. However, without fail, around the two-hour mark of the game, the stadium would almost instantly become 50 percent empty (or 50 percent full?). Ultimately, that was the question Cole and his team had to answer.

His team saw the empty stands, and it made them furious. They blamed the fans. The fans were wrong. The fans needed to wake up and start drinking more Kool-Aid.

But Cole didn't see it that way. Instead, he saw the reality of the half-empty stadium. Even though the experience was fun, the fact that so many people left early meant the Savannah Bananas were doing something wrong. Despite the Bananas continuously upping the bar for their fans with crazy, fun, and hilarious forms of entertainment like throwing out a banana as the first pitch or employing a break-dancing first base coach, after about two hours, the fans were dunzo.

Jesse Cole is a Walt Disney FANATIC. He's read every book and taken trips to Disney World to study the business of the magic they create. He was also mesmerized by P.T. Barnum and used his concept of creating a circus as inspiration as he built his baseball team. A student of innovation, Cole is one of the most disciplined innovators you'll ever witness. As of September 2023, he's written three books outlining his frameworks, routines, and relentless focus on putting fans first and "plussing," which was Disney's term for never being satisfied with your last great idea and delivering more than the customer expects.

But despite Cole and the Bananas' non-stop innovation, they were still missing the mark. Fans leaving before the baseball "show" had ended indicated to him that despite their success, they still weren't fully putting their fans first.

Running a business with customers is cool, but running a business that creates superfans is the real jewel.

The fact of the matter was that Jesse Cole had a huge, seemingly impossible headwind to fight through, which is that baseball is inherently slow. And even when you throw a Mad Hatter tailcoat suit on it, at some point, people get bored and are ready to move on.

But what could he do? Baseball has been around since the mid-19th century. When you research its history (but you don't have to because I did), you'll see that the biggest changes to baseball in its 100-plus-year history are things like what statistics they track, the size of the strike zone, and the height of the pitcher's mound. The average MLB game lasts over three hours. The fact remains that, for the most part, baseball has been played the same way for well over a century.

Pitcher throws the ball.

Batter doesn't swing.

Wait.

Take a sip of beer.

Wait.

Batter adjusts his junk.

Wait.

Batter loosens his glove's Velcro and then puts it back into place.

Wait.

Batter loosens his *other* glove's Velcro and then puts that one back into place.

Wait.

Take another sip of beer.

Batter steps up to the plate.

Pitcher looks at first base.

Wait.

Pitcher throws the ball.

Batter fouls the ball.

Wait.

Wait.

Wait . . .

(And if you're like me, add a step where you check your cell phone at the exact moment someone *finally* hits the ball.)

Despite the Savannah Bananas creating fantastic entertainment to fill as many "Wait" spaces as possible, after a couple hours, even that got old. Cole was resolved to put the team's fans fully first, so he and his team sat down to devise a plan to do just that.

What did they come up with? Oh, you know, just a simple plan that would reinvent about half of the very game that hadn't been reinvented, ever. Not to mention, they would have to do this as a collegiate-summer-league-with-zero-clout team, knowing there was little chance anyone would follow. And since they still wanted it to be a game, well, yeah, they kinda needed at least one other team to follow.

Cole decided that while their focus on ~25% Ruling the game of baseball was growing their business, they were still failing. In order to commit to their "Fans First" mantra, they would have to take more extreme measures. About 25 percent more.

This realization and resolve were the impetus behind the birth of "Banana Ball," a new version of baseball that the Bananas invented. This new game essentially took the traditional game of baseball and kept the things people liked (hitting balls, running bases, eating hot dogs) but got rid of the things people didn't like (games longer than two hours, batters doing seventeen things in between pitches, long chats between pitchers and coaches).

Banana Ball kept roughly half of traditional baseball and then reinvented the rules for the other half.

For example, the Bananas implemented a change in scoring, where instead of tallying runs throughout the game, each inning is worth one point. They also got rid of traditional walks. Instead of the standard walk to first base, if a batter is pitched four "balls," the batter can take off running as far as they can before every defensive player touches the ball (except the pitcher and catcher), at which point they can try and tag them out. They also put a two-hour limit on the game time (duh) and penalized batters who step out of the batter's box by counting that as a strike.

Banana Ball was introduced in 2020, and people loved it. The Savannah Bananas decided to play this new game while also continuing to play their games in their traditional baseball league. They successfully convinced some other teams to give Banana Ball a chance, such that roughly half of their season was spent playing this more progressive, entertainment-focused Banana Ball game.

They continued to split their time for the next few years, and as they did that, Jesse Cole and his team couldn't miss noticing the stark difference between the two games—regular baseball and Banana Ball. While the former was leaving seats half-empty about three-quarters of the way through the game; the latter was packing the seats to nearly full to the end of the game. They also heard from both fans *and* players that Banana Ball was the most fun they'd had watching, and playing, baseball . . . ever.

I've not only been a "student" of Cole's, reading his *Fans First* book and following his inspiring posts on LinkedIn, but I also had the pleasure of interviewing him in 2022 on our podcast (check out episode 165, "The Savannah Bananas' Fans First Strategy You Can Use for Success"). What I didn't know then, but do now, was that when we spoke, he was in the midst of making a ginormous decision.

He and his team began to ask: *Should they continue playing in their regular league AND playing Banana Ball? Or should they instead fully follow their "fans first" strategy and push their chips—or bananas—all in on Banana Ball?*

This wasn't an easy decision; their league play was their cash cow. Leaving it would put their organization in a pickle, potentially leaving them scrambling between 1st and 2nd base with about 10 players waiting to tag them out.

In what is one of the ballsiest (had to) 50% Rule moves ever, they decided to go all-in on Banana Ball. In fact, about a month after meeting Jesse Cole, he announced that the Savannah

Bananas had decided to leave their standard "day jobs" as a baseball team in the Coastal Plain League so they could pursue their 50 percent dream, 100 percent.

Once you have success with The 50% Rule, don't bluff, flop, or fold. Push your chips all in.

If you know anything about the current-day Savannah Bananas mania, you probably picture that announcement being a celebration—something that reads like the one you'll write when you retire: *See ya, suckers!!! It's been real. It's been fun. But it hasn't been real fun. Now it's time for REAL fun!* But that wasn't how it went. Instead, it was a heartfelt, borderline agonizing post.

They had just publicly announced their plan to their local superfans, many of whom had completely drunk the Savannah Bananas' Kool-Aid (well, probably more like Budweiser) for many years. The same fans who had supported them out of the bowels of the notoriously unsuccessful run of baseball in Grayson Stadium. The same fans who were buying tickets, helping them keep their jobs and feed their families. And their reaction? Many of them were pissed. Like Rachel with the audiobook pissed. And that is no bueno.

In order to pursue their 50% Ruled baseball creation, they essentially had to give the heisman to their other half.

They had to break up. They had to tell them they were more in love with the other "person." It probably felt like the most excruciating episode of *The Bachelor* for Cole and his team. They loved two people. But monogamy was required for true success, and they could only give one of them a banana.

Despite the disappointment of many, the Savannah Bananas announced that 2022 would be their last season of playing "regular baseball" in the Coastal Plains League so they could go all-in on Banana Ball.

After they sat a little while on the proverbial park bench crying alongside their local superfans, repeating, "It's not you, it's us," something happened that was almost as crazy as Prince Charming showing up with Cinderella's lost shoe. The Savannah Bananas shed 50 percent, and almost immediately, they blew up.

In just their first year transitioning to full-time Banana Ball, they sold out every game (and then some—there are MASSIVE waitlists). They've held games at Major League Baseball stadiums. Famous baseball players and singers have, not only attended their games, but asked to collaborate. Brian Littrell of the Backstreet Boys recently sang and played with the Bananas.

Bananaland, a documentary on ESPN+, takes you behind the scenes of the evolving national craze around the team too. And breaking news: the Savannah Bananas now even have an exhibit in the Baseball Hall of Fame!

The success stories, shenanigans, and pure joy from the Bananas don't stop rolling in. If you're not already doing so, I recommend following Jesse Cole on LinkedIn. Or, if you're cooler than me, and Instagram or TikTok are more your jam, check out the Savannah Bananas there.

• • • • • • • • • • • • •

Innovating leads you
to incremental.
The 50% Rule leads you
to monumental.

• • • • • • • • • • • • •

What would it look like if you stopped focusing on innovation and started focusing on creating superfans? What are the rules in your business you're following that make *your* customers less than ecstatic? Are they regulated? Are they simply industry norms? Are they things that are a result of less-than-optimal technology? How could you 50% Rule these things so your customers morph into superfans?

Jesse Cole's *Fans First* book was a game-changer for me. Although our execution is evolving and less than a well-oiled machine, my team and I constantly reference our superfans. We track who they are. We discuss ways we can do more for them. We ask ourselves: *What would surprise and delight them? What can we do that would make them become even super-er fans?*

Experiment with ways you might transition your business's attention away from metrics, profits, and sales and instead turn it to applying The 50% Rule to enable creating superfans. Where are your customers' biggest pain points in their interactions with you? How can you 50% Rule that process to create a more authentic experience?

And it's important to remember that 50%ing things so you create superfans doesn't mean you have to offer circus-level experiences. Buc-ee's gas stations are known for their cult following. Although it's easy to think they created *their* superfans because of their amazing food and fun merch, their success all started because they first focused on providing their customers with something much more basic: clean and abundant bathrooms.

Enact The 50% Rule to help you focus on creating, nurturing, and giving your superfans what they want, even if it feels like their "want" is ridiculous. And yes, those metrics, profits, and sales will most certainly fall in line. Well, if the Savannah Bananas are any indication, they'll actually do more than fall in line. They'll get knocked out of the park.

REAL PEEPS STORY

BUSINESS SUCCESS & BEYOND

Like John Madden, Bill McCormick's next career move was obvious. And like Madden, he initially avoided it.

Bill is a veteran of the LinkedIn training space. However, when he decided to go out on his own, he initially steered clear of that route. He felt his point of view differed from many others. At the same time, he wasn't sure he was "right."

In 2017, he decided to push past his doubts and the imposter syndrome he felt, and launched his first LinkedIn training business. He sold training videos modeled after another person's "system" without any deviation. He didn't have much success. Instead of giving up altogether, though, he decided to double down on his 100 percentness by joining forces with someone to become a trainer of *her* LinkedIn "system." While they had some success, he became increasingly frustrated that he couldn't add his own ideas and perspective. His POV continued to quietly stir inside of him.

When he heard about The 50% Rule early on in the book-writing process and joined my collaboration team, something changed. He felt both the comfort of The Rule (take 50 percent of what's worked for others) and the corresponding carefreeness of The Rule (but change the other 50 percent to be *your* ideas). Bill says, "The 50% Rule and its effects on my life have been my ability to truly embrace being a business owner who runs, operates, and works on my own. This has led to me having the best year of my business-owning life. I've added a number of new clients that I'm continuing to build relationships with, as well as expanding into a very pros-pect-rich territory where I have the opportunity to be the only trainer of my kind."

And that's what it's all about, right? Big business success. Whenever Bill would speak up at our collaboration meetings about how much his business continued to soar due (in part . . . probably 50 percent) to The 50% Rule, it lit me up. But I didn't know how much The Rule impacted him in ways that went well beyond business success.

Bill says, "Beyond the financial and business success, The 50% Rule has given me the confidence to believe in myself and bring my POV front and center. I've also started writing my own book, *The Social Sales Compass*, which encourages salespeople to get out of their echo chambers and embrace new and different sales methodologies."

Wait, that's still not even the best part.

Bill says, "The 50% Rule has also had an impact on my personal life. Having been a conservative Christian much of my adult life, I've recently begun reading books from a more liberal perspective as I've sought to understand how to better love and serve people. This has led to a vast change in my beliefs where I value people over theologies and have embraced a human-first outlook, confronted my own entitlement, and I now proudly wear the label of being 'woke.' All of this stems back to a 50% Rule outlook—we have access to knowledge we're given and taught, but we also have experience and our own reason to come to conclusions that are unique to us and to our environment. Understanding this should make us more tolerant of the views of others, especially those whom we don't agree with."

Man-oh-man, that is a link to The 50% Rule that goes beyond my wildest dreams.

20

Halfsies Your Humility

It was 1960, and the American economy was booming. People were still in their post-WWII drunken stupor, buying things like crazy, especially new cars. Detroit was the mega-center for the coolest, most stylish, and elite cars you could get. Every new model seemed to outdo the one before it. Buying a new, American-built car was a status symbol. And marketers kept fueling that status engine.

So, how did a huge underdog car—small, awkward, and German-made—cut through the status symbol mania and become a smash hit? They went halfsies with humility.

But before I tell that story, I wanna take a step back and give you the research behind what makes 50% Ruling humility a powerful strategy. In 1966, psychologist Elliott Aronson had a theory. He thought that people who were considered "superior" (we'll call them "competent" going forward) were more likable and thus more successful when they committed a pratfall. "Pratfall" is an old-fashioned word for someone making some kind of blunder or exposing an imperfection. I call it a humility moment.

To study his theory, Aronson gathered almost fifty college students and asked them to listen to people who were *supposedly* auditioning for a television game show. The applicants were divided into four different groups. 1) competent, no pratfall; 2) competent, with a pratfall; 3) less competent, no pratfall; 4) less competent, with a pratfall. For the experiment, the pratfall was the applicant saying they spilled coffee on their new suit at the end of the recorded interview.

The college students were then asked to answer a survey that included how likable the participant was. What Aronson found, as he suspected, was that those who were presented as competent were MORE likable when they committed a pratfall than those who did not. However, this was not the case for those who were less competent. The pratfall actually made them LESS likable.

What this experiment tells us is that if you're not a nincompoop—you do your job well, you're smart, reliable, your product is good, etc.—then adding in something where *you* expose that you're not perfect makes you more likable. And here's the thing that's really important here. Someone doesn't *find* the imperfection. You expose it. Not because you *have* to, but because you *want* to. Because you're brave enough, generous enough, or vulnerable enough to bring it to the surface.

This is precisely the strategy that Volkswagen took when it introduced its Beetle car to Americans in 1960. They knew they had a major uphill battle to sell into the U.S. market. Volkswagen worked with the marketing firm Doyle Dane Bernbach (DDB) to develop a marketing strategy that wouldn't replicate the trend du jour, i.e., showing the Beetle as a status symbol. Instead, they decided to go halfsies on humility. They 50% Ruled—half humility, half competence—their ad campaign.

They chose to lead with the car's flaws. Instead of pretending the car was cool or perfect, they exposed its flaws purposefully. For example, one of their ad headlines was "Lemon" (slang for a defective product) with the tagline *One of the nice things about owning it is selling it.* At first glance, it seems to the consumer that VW is saying their cars are no good. Anyone paying attention (aka, a potential buyer), though, would think, *That can't be right. VW can't be saying their car is a "lemon."* Then they'd read the rest of the ad copy. Lo and behold, the ad didn't go on about how bad the car was. Instead, the ad displays competency by talking about how one of the Beetles *was* in fact a "lemon"— there was a blemish on the glove box—but never made it past the factory floor since one of Volkswagen's many inspectors caught it. They claimed that their intensive quality review process increased the car's resale value.

Another campaign slogan was *It's ugly but it gets you there.* Instead of pretending like the Beetle was sleek and sexy, Volkswagen went right at the thing consumers were probably already thinking. But they say it first. That holds weight. That is unexpected. That creates trust. That makes them more likable.

Volkswagen isn't the only company to use this strategy, and it's not just a strategy for use in proactive marketing. 50% Ruling your humility and your competence is a great way to recover from making a mistake. That's what Kentucky Fried Chicken (KFC) did in 2018 when it faced a massive chicken shortage. Instead of hiding it or being all snoozy mea culpa-y, KFC ran ads that rearranged "KFC" to "FCK." They didn't hide their blunder. They exposed it in can't-miss-it fashion. But again, only 50 percent. The ads then went on to authentically explain the situation and what (competent) things they were doing to fix it.

With a picture of the famous bucket with "FCK" on it, the ad said, "A chicken restaurant without any chicken. It's not ideal. Huge apologies to our customers, especially those who travelled out of their way to find we were closed. And endless thanks to our KFC team members and our franchise partners for working tirelessly to improve the situation. It's been a hell of a week, but we're making progress, and every day more and more fresh chicken is being delivered to our restaurants. Thank you for bearing with us."

By the way, wouldn't you die to get to work with the lawyers who approved of them going out with such humility and authenticity? (Save this example for the next time you want to do something similar and get the evil eye from your overlords.)

When you smash together humility and competency, humor and facts, apologies and authenticity, there is nothing more powerful. In fact, I've been teaching this concept for years. I know its profound impact firsthand.

One of the things I'm passionate about is that authenticity isn't just fluff. It's work. It's actionable. You have to consciously work hard to fight against the standard inauthentic practices that plague the business world. One of the ways I demonstrate its tangibility and 50% Rule humility and competence is through an exercise I call "Crafting Your Intriguing Intro." It's hands-down the most powerful, favorite, ah-ha moment that happens when I do my authenticity workshops.

The Intriguing Intro is intended to replace the dull, snoozy introductions that you (and others—you're not alone) do when you're being interviewed, introducing yourself in a business meeting, meeting one-on-one with a new colleague, etc. Most introductions go something like this, "Hi, my name is Erin, and

I spent the first ten years of my career at XYZ Company doing project management. And then I came to ABC Company and moved into a marketing role, and . . ." Lost ya yet? Probably. And everyone else, every time you introduce yourself.

Instead, if you 50% Rule humility and competence, you'll wake people up. They'll be leaning in and smiling with an immediate boost to their feelings of connection and trust.

When I work with teams, I simply have each participant spend about a minute writing down a few humility moments—stories of times when they did something wrong, asinine, etc. It can be work-related or not. Then, they spend another minute writing down a "big brag" or two—those career big moments that highlight their competence.

I then ask for volunteers to share their humility and competency components, and I show them how they can piece the two together while capping it off with a *what's in it for them*, that is, why their introduction matters to the person or people they're talking to.

Here's one example: I was working with a leadership team, and the sales leader told us his humility moment was that he made many mistakes when he was first in leadership at a different company. He thought his role was all about what you know, and he failed to relate to his people. He then told a story about how, during that time, he decided to learn how to become a soccer referee, a sport he didn't know much about. That experience humbled him and forced him to reflect on the importance of understanding where his people struggled and how to help them grow. His big brag was that he grew his next sales organization from less than $500,000 in sales to over $6.5 million.

I helped him outline a new Intriguing Intro that said something like this: "Hi, my name is Dude. One important thing to know about me is that I haven't always been a great leader. Earlier in my career, I was that cool, confident guy. That guy who didn't always slow down to connect with my team. Ask questions. Relate. And I had some success, but nothing amazing. And then, when I was forty years old, I decided to get my soccer referee license. In that process, I had an awakening. I realized that we're all constantly learning. That people need support when they're growing and doing new things. I took those lessons with me to my next role, and under this newfound leadership, we grew sales from less than $500,000 to over $6.5 million. I tell you all this because if you work with me, you won't get perfection. You won't get bravado. You'll get someone who truly understands the power of connection, patience, and learning."

I've now done this exercise with thousands of people. Each time, we find powerful new intros for them. We hear and FEEL the power of 50% Ruling humility and competence. We cannot believe the stark difference between that and the "normal" introduction. People feel more confident, inspirational, and significant. And their customers, prospects, and clients feel it too.

Where can you 50% Rule humility and competence? Is it in *your* new introduction? Is it in your team meetings when you introduce the meeting? Is it on your company's website? Is it in your monthly "memos" to your team? Is it in your response to Requests for Proposals (RFP)?

It doesn't have to be huge. It doesn't have to be all "FCK," in-yo'-face stuff. It just has to be a bit unexpected. It just has to expose something of you, your company, or your product that you don't *have* to expose, but you decide to do anyway. You expose it sincerely and then smash it together with your badass business self.

Use your humility to get people to trust you . . . to even root for you. Then give them the good stuff. The information and confidence that you do great things. That you have their back. That your shit is amazing. Much like a dog taking a pill, if you wrap your competence up in peanut butter (i.e., humility), it'll go down so much smoother.

Don't be a FCKing chicken. Give it a try.

21

Cut the Shit

A few weeks ago, my phone lit up. It wasn't good.

There were massive layoffs—5,000 people to be exact(ish)—at my former parent company. It was the largest sweeping "reduction in staff" they had done to date, and several of my friends, colleagues, and clients were impacted. It was one of those layoffs where talent, experience, and contribution had NOTHING to do with whether you were kept or cut.

I used to be part of these kinds of discussions. The brutal conversations executives are forced to have every month on what actions they need to take to "hit the numbers" . . . do whatever it takes.

Every year that I worked the corporate executive beat, it felt like I was swimming in an ocean with my bathing suit on both inside-out AND backward, running on an underwater treadmill, trying to keep my head above water just enough to breathe. Each year, I would proclaim to myself and close colleagues, "This HAS to be the worst year ever. It can't possibly get worse." But it always did. Do less with more was the constant, unspoken mantra. There were days when it felt like I was running our hyper-speed business using a dial-up internet connection. Maddening!

Running a financially successful business is simple math. There is revenue, and there is expense. Your goal is to grow the former and reduce the latter. Most often, the biggest expense is people. So, when times get tough, and you're not growing revenue, cutting people is often the first place leaders look.

But what if the first cut that leaders look to wasn't people? What if, instead, they looked to cut the bullshit? That is, what if your drumbeat to The 50% Rule marched you to first think about whether you could solve the problem by cutting out about half the waste—the unnecessary processes, formalities, spreadsheets, meetings, corporate trainings, etc.—that would free up the time of your people so they *could* do more with less? What if the "less" in that "more with less" mantra actually meant less BS work and not less people?!

Until now, we've focused our 50% Rule discussion on cutting out approximately 50 percent of the things you don't necessarily like, agree with, or are just plain outdated. But what if you, as the leader I know you are, got bolder? What if instead of going through the motions and allowing the BS to roll downhill, you got out a massive pooper-scooper and stopped it from rolling?

What if The 50% Rule was an ongoing mantra that helped you and your team constantly evaluate what is bogging you down and what is unnecessary, EVEN IF IT'S ALWAYS BEEN DONE THAT WAY? If you stop and think about it for a hot second, most wasteful work isn't required. It's regurgitated.

People simply feel pressured to repeat unnecessary things, fearing that not doing them will make them look bad. The definition of *regurgitate*, by the way, is to repeat information without analyzing or comprehending it. (This is the second definition, right after the one about throwing up food.) Take fancy, long, and complex PowerPoint presentations, for example: These became insanely prolific at the company I worked for. Nobody *told* us we had to do them (well, our boss might have, but only because that's what they always saw done), but not doing them made you look like you were doing something wrong.

It's like FOMO on fire. And someone—why not you?—needs to put that inferno out.

Most wasteful work isn't required. It's regurgitated.

In January 2023, Shopify took a massive step towards cutting out unnecessary work for their employees. Instead of cutting people, they cut out meetings. Like, *dramatically* cut out meetings. They refer to their strategy as "useful subtraction." Useful subtraction, 50% Rule. Tomato, tomahto.

Whatever you call it, it was brilliant. Shopify's first step was to develop a bot that could automagically reduce meetings. It marched its cute little bot butt into employees' calendars, aimed its laser beam at them, and deleted any recurring meetings with three or more attendees.

But they also got practical with their cut. They 50% Ruled it. They went in strong but also made room for practicality. For example, they told employees to wait two weeks—sleep on it—then if they still needed those meetings, they could reschedule them. They also implemented a no-Wednesday meeting policy, so everyone has one day each week with the same reprieve to focus, innovate, and jam out on the work they were actually hired to do.

Overall, employees loved it. Shopify's COO, Kaz Nejatian, said an engineer marveled that the new policy allowed them to finally work on what they were primarily hired for: writing code all day.

This initial wave of 50%ing their meetings resulted in Shopify deleting over 300,000 hours of meetings from approximately 10,000 employees' calendars. Nejatian the Negator said the cuts were the equivalent of Shopify adding about 150 employees. Imagine that? Rather than cutting employees, Shopify focused on cutting out the waste their employees deal with so they *could* do more with less!

But you'd be wrong if you think they stopped there. They didn't let the pendulum swing back to normal. Nejatian the Negator teamed up with his colleague Shopify CFO Jeff Hoffmeister. Nejatian and the Calcmeister worked together to increase their meeting warfare by developing a "Meeting Cost Calculator" that was integrated into employees' Google calendars.

The calculator uses data related to potential attendees' job level, the average salary of that job level, and the duration of the meeting to estimate the cost of each meeting. It gives people the sticker price before they shop. It holds up a warning label that shouts like your stingy grandparent, "You damn well be sure the info/decision/outcome you're seeking is worth this much!"

Not only did employees love this meeting buzz cut but Wall Street did also; Shopify's stock price roughly doubled over the next year!

It's genius, AND it's unbelievable that it took someone this long to do this. When I worked in healthcare, the big revolution in the early 2000s was creating tools that provided "price transparency" on the cost of healthcare for consumers. It's about time someone created cost transparency for meetings.

This information matters. I know how powerful meeting cost transparency can be. My company, b Authentic Inc, is supported by a team of part-time, freelance team members. Because I pay them an hourly rate, when I call a meeting, I easily know how much that meeting will cost me. If we have critical things to discuss, we'll hold the meeting. But we often forego them if they're not essential. I save money. They get time back to do the real work they love to do.

What other BS at work needs a cost estimator? Meetings are low-hanging fruit. Can *you* be the next Negator or Calcmeister?

For example, can you lead the charge to calculate the cost of reorganizations? How much time (i.e., money) is wasted when employees stop projects, spend time impressing a new boss, and spend hours figuring out who the new decision-makers are?

How about the cost associated with unnecessary corporate training requirements? Sure, you want to mitigate your risk by ensuring your employees understand basic codes and ethics, but have you ever looked at these programs to see if you can 50% Rule them?

Or what about the worst offender I experienced, PowerPoint? What is the cost associated with someone sitting in their bed until 11:30 p.m., changing fonts and adding cute charts? You might think the answer is "nothing" 'cause they're salaried. But let me tell you, that is WRONG.

In 2004, a leader with intelligence *and* cojones 50% Ruled their company's BS. He sent an email that said, "I'm banning Power-Point presentations from all future meetings. Instead, I want you to write memos."

He loathed PowerPoint presentations. First of all, he thought they came across as passive. He hated that people would focus on a document instead of connecting with each other. And he thought they often were too flashy and lacked clarity. But he didn't ban documents 100 percent; instead, he asked for written memos. He still wanted people to spend time outlining their thoughts and ideas. He saw value in preparation and documen-tation, but not in unnecessary arts and crafts.

Almost twenty years later, Amazon still uses memos instead of internal presentations. When asked about his policy, Jeff Bezos said, "This is the smartest thing we ever did at Amazon." And Lord Al-mighty, Amazon has certainly done some pretty smart things.

If you want to be a *good* leader, focus on adding value. If you want to be a *great* leader, focus on cutting bullshit.

What things can you take the lead on cutting out? And don't give me any of this crap about these ideas having to come from the Jeff Bezos of your company. Authenticity is a circular refer-ence, and when you enact The 50% Rule to cut things out, you're practicing a key quality of authentic leadership. When you have the guts to do tiny acts of rebellion, you'll be amazed at how many others find solace in your authenticity and feel empowered to do the same, both up and down the food chain.

- If you're in Technology, what cost calculators or other bots can you quietly develop and pilot for your team, then roll out to your business partners?

- If you're in Finance, stop beating leaders over the head for savings and start helping them build the business case for reducing BS work.

- If you're in Sales . . . never mind, you don't do any BS work because you don't have time for that. You're off selling.

- If you're in Product, how can you collaborate with your stakeholders using fewer meetings but with more creativity?

- If you're in Operations, can you partner with your Finance friends to find internal efficiencies and pilot those across your company?

- If you're the CEO, take a damn stance. Understand what bogs people down (c'mon, you have a clue—you weren't *always* the CEO) and cut. the. shit.

You're more than a meeting, prettier than a PowerPoint, better than the BS.

Now, go help others do more by helping them do less.

22
Keep Your "I" on the Ball

"Perfection is achieved not when there is nothing more
to add, but when there is nothing left to take away."
~Antoine de Saint-Exupéry

I gotta be honest, this was the hardest chapter for me to write.
I wrote more iterations of it than any other in this book, but I
couldn't leave you hanging. I need to support you, the employee who sometimes feels like a cog, the one who's part of that
large, bureaucratic organization. Sometimes you can't just innovate on your own; sometimes the parameters are a little more
complex. I knew I had to give you The 50% Rule (I)nnovation
Framework.

I've been an entrepreneur for all the years I have been beating
the 50% Rule drum. While I've seen plenty of evidence of this
simple rule propelling complex innovation, I know things get
much more complicated when working in larger teams and
organizations.

I mean, I wasn't born yesterday. For twenty-two years, I bopped around a Fortune 50 company where "matrixed" was less like a cool Keanu Reeves movie and more like one of those pirate-ship-esque rope walls you have to climb up, foot over foot, but get stuck, twisted, and annoyed every time you take a step. There are many cooks, taste testers, and food critics in the kitchen. They all have to be involved in innovation in a big company. Putting a positive spin on it, it's a team sport to innovate and move forward. I need to arm your team with a teensy bit more than just The 50% Rule.

This is why I took a step back and, in a dramatic, bullet list move, analyzed what goes through our minds when we execute The 50% Rule to innovate.

Up until now, we've reveled in its simplicity, but is there something more complex that underlies its effect? And how can a bigger team, group, or company use the underlying steps as a more substantial framework for innovation?

And that's how The 50% Rule (I)nnovation Framework[3] was born:

1. Inventory—how is it done today?
2. Intent—why is it done?
3. Investigate—what do you like/what works? What don't you like/doesn't work?
4. Inspire—what are some non-related things that you like?
5. Integrate—merge the old way with some new ways.
6. Invent—name, position, and market your innovation.

---

3. *You can download a one-sheet guide for the (I)nnovation Framework at* the50percentrule.com.

If you break down The 50% Rule and its throughlines as demonstrated in the book, you'll see these six steps play out. Here's a more detailed outline of how you can put this framework into action:

1. The Rule requires you to **inventory** how things are done today. This is part of the "don't throw the baby out with the hot tub water" lesson. We don't want to be idiots and not use some baseline best practices. For example, I needed to understand all the standard steps and processes for creating the audiobook version of *You Do You(ish)*. You might recall that starting from scratch with complete rebellion would have pissed off Rachel and a lot of other "Rachels."

   → Have your group first brainstorm a list of current practices. This will probably feel a bit slow and annoying to some at first, but stick with it. Press them to unearth the industry and/or your company's best practices. This is a great warm-up exercise to get the juices flowing. It also helps the team see just how many places there's an opportunity for innovation. Jesse Cole and his baseball team didn't start with reinventing an entirely new game called Banana Ball; they started with the status quo, and then every week, at every step, they made it better.

2. Next, it's important to understand the **intent** of those current practices. Understanding the steps in the status quo's "why" is essential so that when you decide to replace ~50 percent of the current things, you'll likely keep the intent the same but develop a different approach/strategy/step to achieving that intent.

→ You'll want to revisit each of the current steps and processes and write down the intent of each. For example, is
the step to collect information? If so, what is the purpose
of gathering that information? I encourage you to think
through each step, zoom out, and understand the bigger
picture. *Is the current process intended to make the customer feel more at ease? Gain their attention and trust?
Make them aware of something important?*

For example, if Lin-Manuel Miranda was going through
this exercise, he would ask his team what the intent of a
Broadway show's music was, and they would probably
say: to tell a story and create a vibe. That might lead
them quickly to say that the vibe they want to create is
best supported by hip-hop. This is a lot different than
starting with the standard Broadway "playbook" and
then feeling extra weird when you randomly decide to
use a different kind of music without dialogue. When
you understand the intent, the answer is often more obvious and feels less weird.

3. The third step is to **investigate**, i.e., determine what is just
fine about how things are done today and what things aren't
so fine. Too often, we pooh-pooh the status quo based on
how the current flow makes us feel. That was my experience
with audiobooks. Because most audiobooks felt inauthentic
and made me tune out, my initial thought was to scrap that
shit altogether. But when I finally slowed my roll and thought
about what I liked and didn't like, it allowed me to 50%
Rule it instead of going rogue and landing myself in the
Worst Audiobook Hall of Fame.

→ Go through your list and have people identify those steps that feel like they work . . . or maybe even that *can't* be changed. Then, identify those that feel awkward, don't work well, or are ripe for innovation. When John Madden was trying to decide if he wanted to go into broadcasting or not, at first, it was a "hell no" because he looked quickly at the big picture of broadcasting, and he didn't like it. But perhaps as Madden broke broadcasting down into pieces he realized that he loved for a game to be commentated (and he certainly LOVED football). He just didn't like the language, energy, and lack of teaching part of the process currently in place at CBS. He went on to do broadcasting, keeping the overall intent, but changing up some of the "how."

4. The fourth step, **inspire**, is the most fun, and it's the most difficult. You can certainly brainstorm this in a meeting, but I might suggest this is also ripe for "homework" for the team. This step is where the mixology comes in. You want to look to other best practices and ideas from places far and wide. Ideas could come from new products in different markets, podcasts, an article you read . . . anywhere. Say I'm looking into what our team can learn from the most successful cookie-selling Girl Scouts, and what from their strategy we might be able to use to help sell this book. I mean, if I have to pop a tent at the intersection of a Dunkin' and a Chick-fil-A to sell this thing, let's GO!

→ Help your team talk through the intent behind the areas you marked as ripe for change and innovation. Where have they seen someone execute a similar intent but in a totally different way? For example, what great experiences have people had when they travel? How might something experienced while traveling be applied to one of your current services or steps? What idea might have come about from a podcast someone recently listened to? What recent commercial totally caught your eye and wallet? What about it captivated you, and how could you use that in your product or service?

Important note: Condition the team that most of these ideas should come from their personal experiences, books, articles, etc., and NOT from the industry you serve. Remember, juxtapositions create joyful jolts. And innovation.

5. Now it's time to **integrate** the old with the new. Start by focusing on just one thing; you don't have to achieve 50% Ruling right out of the gate. What is the best idea your team came up with that can be implemented relatively easily? Try to steer clear of the ideas that will take three years and $20 million of IT funding to complete. For example, Jesse Cole and the Savannah Bananas started with the entertainment they provided fans. Later, they would implement more complex things like an all-you-can-eat ticket pricing scheme and unique, customized outreach to fans. But they first tackled the thing they thought most needed solving—fans' boredom while players spent sixty seconds adjusting their nether regions.

    → List all your ideas from Step 4 and have the team vote on the one they think is best. That's all I got for this one.

6. Lastly, you need to mark this as **innovation**. I could have simply left things at "integrate" and implied innovation, but

the final step in innovation is to ensure people see what you're doing as innovation. Too often, people don't fully step into the limelight with 50% Ruled innovation because it feels too easy. We have this disease, or maybe just insecurity, that the only things we get to market as "innovation" come after implementing a $100 million IT project or creating a new, never-been-seen service. Before, you might have emailed your clients or merely talked about it in a finalist presentation, and that was it. Now we're going to own our innovation. You need to splash this 50% Rule (I)nnovation out there like a motha!

→ The last step should be to develop branding for your innovative new product or service. Don't hold back on naming your new masterpiece. And nothing is too small to name (I mean, look how many things I put names to in this book). Naming isn't just a marketing tool; it helps people remember and relate to something. It also sparks additional innovation.

For example, if you went ahead with the idea I threw out in Chapter 18, sending your new customers a DoorDash gift card to support your new client's tech onboarding process, you might refer to this little service as your "No Tech Goes Hangry" product. The fun part is that once you name it, it creates a theme that will likely catalyze other creative ideas. Now that you have your "hangry" theme, that might also give you the idea to send Snickers bars to your clients every time you have a new product upgrade that needs to be installed, with instructions wrapped around the bar.

When innovation adopts a theme, your team's imagination will be ignited to create branches off that theme, which creates an organic, non-stop innovation engine!

The next time you're handed a manual, playbook, or system that feels less than optimal, stop, drop, THINK, and *then* roll. Ask, "What is the intent of this process? What is this trying to achieve?" Don't just look at it as a whole. Break down the steps. What is the intent of each step? Is there a better way to do them? Is there a way to redo that step so you're more likely to love doing it and thus stick with it?

Experiment with the framework. Adjust. Add. Get feedback. Use it again. Hell, feel free to sick your Six Sigma ninja self on the 50% Rule (I)nnovation Framework. And if you do, post your (I)nnovation story on LinkedIn and tag me @Erin-Hatzikostas. Let me, and the world, know how you jazzed it up!

P.S. For this chapter, I took a play from the last one and cut the shit; I initially wrote a story to start this chapter off like I often do, but I realized it just didn't serve you. This also wasn't the first time I "cut the shit" from the book. I wrote several other stories but then decided they weren't all that helpful. Other sections that fell to the cutting room floor include a story about how Ed Helms's real-life missing tooth helped him land his epic role in *The Hangover*; a story about negotiating from the book *Never Split the Difference*; and even my one of my favorite stories about the former L.A. Rams' star, Jalen Ramsy, and his relationship with the Rams' 50% Ruled mariachi band. Less is almost always more.

SECTION 5:

. . . .

50% YOUR PERSONAL LIFE

23
Reinvent Your Relationships

It was August 2018, and a month earlier I had announced my retirement from my corporate CEO position. For the five years up to that point, Manny and I had a part-time nanny helping us out. My husband commutes one hour each way to work, and as our kids got bigger, and so did my job, we realized we HAD to have support to make it all work.

One of the things we don't talk enough about are the practical, tangible steps women can take to help us say "yes" to the big-girl job. For me, one of those things was using a service called Care.com. When we were faced with the conundrum of how we'd make it all work, this matchmaking site was clutch. Over the course of six years, we had four amazing women support our family on a part-time basis, all found via Care.com.

Back to that day in August: Our current part-time nanny had recently gotten engaged. Her fiancé was in the Navy and was re stationed to New Hampshire, so we sadly had to part ways.

I posted a new job on Care.com, and a few weeks later, I found a great candidate. One evening, I told my husband we were going to interview someone for the nanny position. He was like, "Huh?! You are retiring in a few months. Why would we hire someone new?"

Yes, I *was* retiring. But not entirely. I had plans to start something new (I didn't know quite yet that it would be my speaking and business coaching business, b Authentic Inc). And I knew a few things: a) we still had a LOT to juggle in the next few months, and b) I was going to continue to work. I just didn't quite know exactly what that would look like. Not having any support was frightening. But hiring someone, not knowing what the future held, was also frightening.

I explained my feelings to Manny, and he agreed that we should go ahead with bringing in someone new. Our biggest concern wasn't us; it was hiring someone and not being able to fulfill our commitment to them.

We met a young woman named Kaitlyn Czapiga. She was pure joy . . . the perfect energy and fit for what we were looking for in another part-time nanny. We were open to her about our situation. I told her, "I'm going to continue to work, but I'll be honest, I'm not entirely sure what support we'll need with the kids. I'll have more time and flexibility than before. But I also want help, so I'm not forced to hold back from fully pursuing my next venture."

And then, with little thought, I spewed out a 50 percent question/50 percent statement. "Maybe you can help me with my business too?" Kaitlyn immediately said "Sure!" to the crazy, ill-defined, clearly-gonna-change arrangement I tossed her way. And what happened after that was pure magic.

When I officially retired from my corporate job, Katilyn and I 50% Ruled our relationship. She still helped out with the kids from time to time. I also "traded in" kid-watching time for business-helping time. For example, I talked in Chapter 7 about how she helped me create and record my online course, *b Brilliant: From Passed By to Promoted.*

Did she know what she was doing? Nope. But neither did I. Plus, she contributed something WAY more important than rules and playbooks. She contributed energy. She brought excitement. Whenever I told her about a new idea or breakthrough, she was genuinely giddy. Even though she was only twenty-three, that girl propelled me more than any $80,000 coach or $100,000 mastermind.

Several years later, one of the most surprising benefits from our 50% Ruled relationship was that Kaitlyn also learned a lot about entrepreneurship via this pseudo-apprenticeship we had stumbled into. She went on to start her own business—Soul Magic—a holistic wellness business that offers services like regression hypnosis, Reiki energy healing, and spiritual life coaching. But her launching her own business isn't even the best part of this story. The best part was the unlikely and strong friendship we developed. Despite me being twenty-plus years her senior, she and I created a very special relationship.

Find one great person and do two amazing things together.

They should have hated each other. He ruled in favor of stopping the Bush/Gore Florida vote recount. She ruled that the

Supreme Court didn't have the right to intervene. He ruled that a D.C. law banning firearms violated the 2nd Amendment. She ruled to uphold the law. He ruled that Hobby Lobby could restrict paying for contraception for its employees. She wrote a strong dissent, fearing a slippery slope that would impact women's right to reproductive healthcare. (It's like she had a crystal ball.)

Despite being on opposite sides of the aisle on these opinions and many others, U.S. Supreme Court Justices Ruth Bader Ginsburg (RBG) and Antonin Scalia were the best of friends.

They were both born in March, from New York, and short in stature. That was where their similarities, on the surface, ended. But despite being wildly different in opinions and personalities, they formed a precious and profound friendship. Two of the most influential judges in the world found a way to 50% Rule their relationship.

It all started when they were both D.C. Court of Appeals Judges. Justice Scalia loved trying to make Justice Ginsburg laugh while on the bench. Despite their differences, they both formed a deep respect for each other's work.

They soon became friends outside of work. They and their spouses often hung out together, including spending many New Year's Eves together. They also shared a love for the opera, so much so that Derrick Wang created an opera inspired by them, aptly named *Scalia/Ginsburg*. When they went to the theater together, they occasionally both dressed in period clothing/costumes. They even rode on an elephant together in India!

They saw their relationship as 50 percent work, 50 percent human. Justice Scalia once said, "I attack ideas. I don't attack people. And some very good people have some very bad ideas. And if you can't separate the two, you gotta get another day job."

The 50% Rule helps you see friends through a new lens.

As you think about *your* friends, challenge conventional notions of how you interact and live alongside your friends. What if friends could be your companions/roommates for more parts of your life than just your twenties? What if you felt comfortable leaving your house messy when friends came over, or didn't always bring a dish to their party? What if you let your best friend make choices you don't agree with—and what if you didn't pass judgment on them at all?

While Justice Ginsburg and Justice Scalia's opinions sometimes differed, they often gave the other person a heads-up when they knew their views would clash. They knew this would give them more time to digest it and form the most well-thought-out counter-opinion. In fact, Justice Ginsburg said they would even pass along suggestions on how they could make each other's opinions clearer, even when they were in opposite "courts."

When Justice Antonin Scalia passed away in 2016, Ginsburg told one of her favorite stories from her time with Scalia at his funeral, a story she'd tell again a few months later at the Second Circuit Judicial Conference. She said that when President Clinton was trying to decide on his first nomination for the Supreme

Court, Clinton asked Justice Scalia, "If you were stranded on a desert island with your new court colleague, who would you prefer, Larry Tribe or Mario Cuomo?"

She said, "Scalia answered quickly and distinctly: 'Ruth Bader Ginsburg.' Within days, the President chose me."

Gavel (and tear) drop.

REAL PEEPS STORY

TRICK (REALLY) OR TREAT

As Adam Feltes sat on his beautiful, jack o' lantern'd porch, handing out candy, he felt increasingly blah. It was another year of Halloween trick-or-treating. And while he is always up for the fun the day promises, something didn't feel right. Adam said, "It's a holiday. Like many, it has just become so mundane, slanted toward lazy modern traditions, and full of silly expectations: I have a bag. You have a light on. Candy will be exchanged."

Adam started to notice that there was a wide variation in how the kids acted when they came to do the habitual exchange. "In the first twenty minutes, I had experiences that ranged from fabulously polite young people, i.e., said *trick or treat*, chose their favorite snack, thanked us, and wished us a happy Halloween—to the opposite, i.e., walked up, took the candy, and returned to the parents who'd done no coaching. I got the urge to engage more and be part of the tradition AND coach the children."

That's when he decided to shake things up, altering tradition for greater impact. At first, he simply rewarded the well-mannered kids by handing them a second piece of candy. However, he also let those who were less polite know that they missed out. As he put it, "It was a carrot and stick all at once."

He did this for a few minutes when one of the kids, who had been told he missed out on a second piece, was clearly not happy. Adam said, "After a few minutes, a three-foot-tall Pokémon went nuts over his mistake. He practically screamed, 'I always say thank you. I just forgot. Let me make it up to you. I'll do a dance!'" To which Adam replied, "Only if the dance has a cartwheel involved."

What happened next was pretty cool. First, Pokémon went on to coach his sister that if she said thank you, she could also get a second piece of candy. But the inspirational cartwheel didn't stop turning there. "By 7:30, my front yard looked like a gymnasium. The fire truck was parked out front with lights flashing. Parents were shocked the kids didn't want to go get more candy but stayed and played instead."

When Adam decided to 50% Rule his candy-giving approach by adding in new "requirements," his tiny adaptation made a big impact. On the surface, he trained kids to be more polite and created a "party" on his front lawn. But, more than that, he inspired kids to coach *other* kids, AND he gave permission to them, and to others, to do things differently. People have no idea how much they're yearning for something new and different . . . until someone has the guts to do new and different. I'm certain that next year, his neighborhood will be full of other Halloween 50%ing (or even other holidays will be 50%ed), all inspired by his desire to coach the kids and create a new twist on the age-old question: trick or treat?

24

Binary Be Bad

I drove my daughter to school early one morning. When I got back home and went to get out of the car, I screamed out loud, "Oh, my God!!!" Tears started streaming down my face. I had Sleeprunning Syndrome. For real.

Several years earlier, I had injured my back. That was the first time I'd ever had a back injury. It took me months to realize it was caused by a new, at-home, unergonomic chair situation. Public Service Announcement: ergonomics matter.

I was fortunate to get better. But about every nine months after that, I would do something stupid (i.e., deadlift at the gym) and the pain would return. Unfortunately, each time, it got worse.

The last time it flared up, I decided to see a physical therapist (PT). After three months, and what felt like 162 different exercises, I felt much better. "She was a miracle worker!" I boasted to anyone who would listen. Until said miracle expired on that fateful morning when I screamed out in pain and earned myself a trip to the emergency room.

So then, pissed at the apparent ineffectiveness of the PT "miracle worker" and her 162 physical therapy exercises, I decided to see a chiropractor instead. His approach was very different from that of the physical therapist. If you've ever been to both, you know what I mean. Basically, physical therapists think chiropractors are full of shit, and chiropractors think physical therapists are full of shit.

Rather than strengthening the muscles around my back, the chiropractor spent his time manipulating and massaging the pain. He also gave me three or four stretches to do. The physical therapist gave me zero stretches. The chiropractor gave me zero exercises. After my relapse post physical therapy, I was now drinking chiropractor Kool-Aid. PT must have been wrong. Chiro must be right.

I felt like a cat watching a ping-pong match, and for the time being, I was clapping my paws for Team Chiropractor.

But guess what? Yep, several months later, my back was messed up again. WTF?! Who was right? The physical therapist? The chiropractor? Or did no one have the answers needed to solve my back issues?!

(What comes next is a PERFECT example of why I'm *making* you read a whole damn book on this Rule because even the 50% Rule Queen can't get her shit together enough to consistently apply The Rule!)

I realized that I needed to 50% Rule my back pain solution. Here's what I did. Finally.

I realized that out of the 162 physical therapy exercises, there were two exercises that helped most. And out of all the things the chiropractor did and suggested, there were two stretches that also helped. Armed with four things, instead of a gazillion, it quickly became apparent that I could do these four things every day.

If there is one thing more important to 50% Rule than ANYTHING else suggested in this book, it's your health. Why? Because nobody's body responds the same way. Nobody knows your bod better than you. Lastly, nobody is 100 percent right. Not physical therapists. Not chiropractors. Not even brain surgeons. You are the best person to curate your way to better health.

You need to be the proctor of your doctor.

Ever since I finally 50% Ruled my back pain, mixing the two together and curating my own solution, I only see the chiropractor about once a month to keep things in alignment. I start every day, usually before I work out at the gym, with my two chosen stretches. And then, when I do my workout, I substitute two of the day's exercises for the two PT exercises that help me the most. I do this almost every day. In fact, one of the gym coaches told me one day that another member said they noticed I tended to do my own thing often. To which I replied, "You have no idea."

When I talk about Sleeprunning Syndrome, you probably think, "Tee hee hee, that's so cute. Not sure I really have that syndrome, but it's a clever little metaphor." Well, the Sleeprunning I was doing between "back doctors" caused me LITERAL symptoms. I was such an idiot that I even developed a new one— **Binary Bursitis.**

Binary Bursitis happens when you're an ignoramus and believe you must choose one opposing thing over another. You think everything has a right side and a wrong side. And you Sleeprun back and forth between the two, convinced you have to pick one or the other.

What I'm throwing your way goes well beyond your health. There are so many damn things in life that, for some reason, we treat as binary decisions:

- Vegetarian or carnivore: It's actually okay to eat less meat and more veggies. You don't have to declare one or the other. I'm not a vegetarian, but nine times out of ten, I'll pick the veggie burger over a beef one.

- Man or woman: This is the most "main stage" binary discussion going on right now. I have a good friend, Erin Baker (author of *Joy-Full AF*), who chooses not to choose. I fully support them or anyone who decides their gender isn't binary.

- Corporate job or entrepreneur: Mark my words, this binary choice will be massively disrupted in the next twenty years. Companies are seeing the value in moving away from full-time employees (FTE) and hiring freelancers or "fractional" workers, even in senior-level roles. They can be more agile with their workforce, and employees can shed a bunch of the FTE bullshit they can't stand dealing with.

- Family vacation or friend getaway: I bet you never feel like you can go on all the vacations you want to go on, and you sometimes have to choose between family trips and friend getaways. But what if you could do both . . . together? For inspiration, my podcast co-host and good friend, Nicole, traveled to Greece with me and my family this past summer. (Shout-out to the kids' "Auntie Nicole"!) You don't have to choose.

- Democrat or Republican: This binary obsession is doing MUCH more damage than Binary Bursitis. I'll leave this one at that, so you're not tempted to burn my book.

So, ask yourself at every decision point: Does this decision *have* to be binary?

What would you love doing if you didn't have to choose? How might you design your career if binary wasn't even an option? Could you redesign your family and relationships in a better way if you stepped away from standard definitions and modi operandi?

You aren't part of a gang. You don't have to choose to either be Crips or Bloods. You don't have to be a "runner" to run. You don't have to be a "speaker" to speak. You don't have to be a "leader" to lead. You don't have to be an "entrepreneur" to make money on your own. You don't have to be "military" to fight. You don't have to be a "philanthropist" to make an impact. You don't have to be a "writer" to write.

Time to say bye-bye to bye-nary.

Stop picking teams and start crafting your own dreams.

25
Work-Life Win-Wins

Work-life balance [puke]. Work-life integration [hurl]. If you're like me, you're sick of hearing about these elusive concepts. It feels like someone's just trying to put lipstick on Darth Vader.

But lipstick with me here: Can you agree to get curious to see if The 50% Rule is the tactical, practical mantra you need to win your lightsaber battle with "doing it all?"

As I've mentioned, "Discipline" is NOT my middle name. I largely consider myself a "winner" and often work my arse off. But mostly because I'm inspired. When I'm not inspired—Bah humbug! I'm not the girl who's gonna push through the eighty-point checklist because there's supposed success at the end of that hell hole.

But sometimes, I just gots to do the stuff. One of my hacks to do hell-hole tasks is to do them in a new location ("new-lo") . . . preferably one where this is some sort of reward. For example, I used to hate preparing for podcast interviews. It felt like work that slowed me down. Despite knowing how much better the episode would be, I hated doing it.

My go-to, new-lo strategy for this specific hell-hole task is to listen to the guest's previous podcast interviews while I'm running or walking. I find I'm much happier when it feels like I'm killing 100 percent of the birds with 50 percent of the stones.

My other go-to, new-lo strategy is going to Panera Bread. I love me some Panera, and I tend to use this strategy when I need the motivation to write or prepare a presentation. Once I'm settled into the pearly gates of heaven with my "Pick Two: Fuji Apple Salad with Chicken, and Butternut Squash Soup," I feel like a superhero. I crank out chapters. I outline new ideas. I pull together dreaded PowerPoints.

This summer, both my children had summer schoolwork. Ella, my sixteen-year-old, is disciplined and anal-retentive. She's her dad. Mick, my thirteen-year-old son, is unorganized and loves to procrastinate. He *may* be his mom. This summer, when he was tapped to jump up two math levels in 7th grade, he was assigned an online math program to complete over summer. Spoiler alert: drama ensued.

For the first two months of summer, despite having hours on end when he had NOTHING else going on, he didn't touch his math. I dug deep into my soul, and despite wanting to wring his neck, I decided the biggest lesson he needed to learn going into middle school was how to be independent in getting his work done. Or so I thought. I ended up teaching him a different 50% Rule lesson.

Fast-forward to the third week of August and this boy's got a big math hill to climb. Instead of lambasting him, I decided to let him in on my little secret. I told him about my go-to, new-lo strategy for getting stuff done. I then offered to take him to Panera later that week. I told him he could do his math, and I could write. He asked if he could have mac n' cheese. The deal was sealed.

That Friday, we spent about three hours in Panera together. I'm not going to lie; it wasn't entirely a scene from a fanciful movie. (There were definitely times when his out-loud math frustrations were ruining my Zen writing vibes.) But overall, it was a success. He made a big dent in his math work. I got some writing done. But most importantly, I demonstrated to him one technique for supplementing discipline to get things done.

My mind is constantly calibrating how I can 50% Rule something. I'm always looking for alternative pathways to figure out how I can do big, hairy tasks without simply relying on discipline. My 50% Rule conditioning makes it easier and easier for me to come up with ideas like the Erin & Mick New-lo-palooza that allowed us to *both* get work done.

In the past, I would have lamented. I would have declared that work-life was imbalanced because I had work to do, but instead, I had to help my son get his math done. Instead, in this case, I *did* help Mick get his math done. I just 50% Ruled it. He worked + I worked + we both got to eat a yummy lunch.

What *work* things are getting in the way of your *life*? If you have to travel, can you sometimes bring your child(ren) with you? If you have a meeting you have to prep for, can they help give you feedback on it and learn in the process? If you have a big presentation to create, can you create a co-working, new-lo situation like I did with Mick?

What *life* things are getting in the way of *work*? When your mom wants to spend more time with you, can you sit together at Starbucks while she reads and you work? If your daughter has an out-of-state tournament, could you arrange to meet a client from that area for lunch? If you have to go to hockey practice for hours on end, could you write a book? (Ahem, where about 50 percent of this book was written.)

Essentially, can you ditch the concept of work-life balance or integration and instead think more about how 50% Ruling specific moments can create win-wins?

Find work-life win-wins.

After Mick and I had our new-lo rendezvous, I was talking about it to his sister and one of her best friends, Marina. A few days later, Marina asked me, "Can you and I go to Panera one day next week, so I can work on my biology?" "Absolutely," I replied. That next Friday, Marina and I jetted off to Panera and worked together for a few hours. It was heartwarming to know that this 50% Rule work-life hack was that contagious. I hope my kids, Marina, and you will use this strategy for the rest of your lives.

And Mick? Well, it must have rubbed off on him in more ways than one. Since starting his 7th-grade advanced math class, he has regularly done his homework via group calls with his friends. He essentially 50% Ruled my new-lo strategy and took the part about working on things with others as his go-to win-win. In fact, as I'm writing this, I can hear him in his room, non-stop talking, singing, and mathing with his crew.

The 50% Rule is outrageously contagious.

Mick plays hockey, and his home rink is about a thirty-five minute drive from our house. Needless to say, we spend A LOT of
time driving. And Mick loves to talk. One day a few years ago, in
a desperate attempt to get a little reprieve from his jibber-jabber,
I decided to 50% Rule our drive. I played one of my favorite
podcasts, *How I Built This.*

I did this for two reasons. The first was a strategic move to
stop his chatter for a bit. The second reason was that I knew the
podcast's powerful stories from entrepreneurs would probably
impact him someday.

Several years later, we still listen to this podcast together.
About a month ago, we were listening to an episode with the
founder of Kinko's, Paul Orfalea (episode 546, in case you want
to check it out). When the host, Guy Raz, asked him how he was
able to motivate the growing number of Kinko's stores with
seemingly limited corporate infrastructure, Orfalea replied that
he gave them equity. He believed that everything is much easier
if people have a stake in the success.

Fast-forward a few weeks. Mick and I got into a discussion
about college. He talked about how important he thought it was
to know what you want to focus on once you get into college.
Trying to be a cool mom, I countered his point. I told him that
in his twenties it's okay to experiment and take different twists
and turns to see what he really wants to do. I went on to tell him
that I thought there were some classes that just about anyone
could benefit from taking, and marketing was one of those.

Being the contrarian that he is, he argued my point. He said
that he could hire good marketers. I then told him that if he

became an entrepreneur, nobody would care as much as he did about the marketing of this business. And therefore, he probably needed to understand marketing. To which he replied, "Yes, they will. I'll just give them equity."

That little craphead threw The 50% Rule right back in my face. He beat me at my own game. Mick had stored away this important nugget from the Kinko's episode. He mashed it with the traditional views he'd heard from others on the importance of focus in college. Amazing: He curated his own view. Annoying: He was right.

This isn't the first time he's implicitly or explicitly thrown The 50% Rule in my face. He's listening. He's soaking it in. He's got the bug.

That's what I want for you too. Maybe it's your kids. Maybe it's your colleagues. Maybe it's your partner. Talk about The 50% Rule. Even when it seems a stretch, share the love. Share the simple mantra that's a light switch for your brain. Practice it. Demonstrate it. Preach it. Morph it. Share it. Repeat it.

In your life. In your work. Everywhere.

REAL PEEPS STORY
....

NEW MOM BOMB

Shortly after Mari Dertinger had her first daughter, the baby-moon concluded and the darkness set in. Ironically, her life was quickly taken hostage by someone who couldn't even hold her head up. She felt trapped, exhausted, and confused. That is, she felt like just about every *other* mom on the face of this Earth. And, as most of us do, she decided to turn to other moms for their advice. One gave her a book on sleep scheduling. She told Mari it was a lifesaver and she hoped it would be for her too.

Mari recalls, "I devoured the book and then referred to it like a bible at every turn. The book was clear about only letting the baby sleep in the crib and how bad it was to let them sleep in the swing. I read and re-read that paragraph as my daughter slept in the swing—she preferred it—and I cried, already labeling myself a 'horrible' mother after only two months on the job."

The good news is that Mari didn't sit in her baby doo-doo long. She quickly realized that the book was having an unintended *negative* impact on her (and, as a result, her daughter). She says, "I returned the book to my friend after just a week and began to adapt the bits and pieces I remembered to our lifestyle. I did apply principles from the book, not as gospel truth but as more of a foundation to build my parenting style and schedule. It became a tool in my toolbox rather than THE tool."

And how did it work out? Mari recalls, "It worked! She slept through the night at eight weeks, and I went on to use 'my' method to 'sleep train' four other kids, some sleeping through the night as early as six weeks. All my kids were great sleepers, and I never picked up a parenting book again. I fully subscribe to The 50% Rule in parenting, to be the best parent I can be for my children."

But this wasn't just a 50% Rule parenting success story. This experience and her epiphany carried on with her well beyond managing babies. "It was helpful for me as a new mom but even more helpful because it began my journey of giving up my perfectionistic ways and realizing I brought a lot to the table, enough to use a little of someone's advice and then curate the rest."

26

You Do You & Let Them Do Them

My memory sucks. Despite wholesale forgetting vacations I've taken, there are also random, seemingly small moments I somehow vividly recall. Can you relate?

One of those moments was when I was at an internal business conference. Gosh, I used to love going to those things. When I was young and without kids to manage, getting face time with executives felt like spending a day at the Oscars. They were the celebrities of my world. One evening at the conference happy hour, I recall talking to one of those "celebrities."

I only remember one thing from that entire conversation. He told me the key to managing it all was that he and his family always sat around the kitchen table for dinner. I thought, *That's so simple yet also so critical. Got it. Will do.* About twenty years and two kids later, I can't count the number of times I've thought back to his advice and felt like a complete failure.

Dinner? Together? At a table? We haven't done that in four months. My husband doesn't get home until six(ish), and the kids have each had at least one after-school activity by then. Sitting around the table for dinner is often impossible.

But let me admit something: Even if it *is* possible, we rarely do it.

My husband and daughter have slight sensory issues, so hearing others eat (without music or the TV) is tough for them. Sometimes, the kids come home hangry, and I'll make them something before Manny gets home. We rarely get to lounge and relax, so there are other times when a few of us sit at the kitchen island eating while a few sit in the living room.

For years, I quietly noticed this and kept marking *F*s on my parenting scorecard, based on the rubric set by some random celebrity—I mean, sales exec—twenty years ago.

Then, one day, I went back to The 50% Rule (I)nnovation Framework breakdown and realized I never paused to ask myself, *What was the INTENT of his family dinners?* I realized the intent was probably to talk, bond, and stay connected. And then I realized our family doesn't do that through dinners; we do that through sports.

What's your unique family bonding? Is it board games? Is it going for hikes? Is it watching a favorite TV show? I'm sure you have something. And whatever it is, it's amazing. Keep doing it.

For our family, watching sports is everything to us. I'm obsessed with watching sports. Why? I'm pretty sure it all goes back to that authenticity thing. TV shows and movies—in the end, they're fake. Sports? Anything goes. They're authentic as hell. You never know which way things will turn out.

My love has certainly rubbed off on my family. While my husband and son were there with their own intrinsic love, I was determined to not have a daughter who would sit at a Super Bowl party and say, "I don't even understand what a 'down' is. I just like the commercials." Hells to the no. Not my girl!

And it worked. Ella shares our love of sports as well. If you come to our house, there is almost always a sporting event on the TV—NFL football, professional soccer, Grand Slam tennis matches, and our absolute favorite—college basketball.

This is how we bond. We talk about sports. We share updates. We snuggle and watch games. I may even do this weird slap-my-son's-bum ritual as a superstitious thing when we watch the UConn men play basketball. Hmm, he's thirteen years old. That one may need to stop soon.

Other families' rubrics are not yours to keep score.

This seems easy enough, but I want you to count every time over the next two weeks that you "score" your parenting and family based off what you see other families doing. Here are some places you're creating rubrics and might be "keeping score:"

When you notice another family. . .

- Taking a vacation
- Having Sunday dinners

- Going for hikes

- Rescuing puppies

- Running races together

- All sitting on the game sidelines

- Having weekly game nights

- Having weekly date nights

I'm here to tell you that other than the first one, my family doesn't do most of those things. But we do go to the beach together, we have a few annual traditions, we ski together, and we watch sports together.

My friend, YOU CANNOT DO IT ALL. And I'm here to tell you that most families can *barely* do 50 percent of what you consider "traditional" family bonding. The next time you compare yourself to a friend who seems to parent/live/be/do better than you, whip out that SWOT analysis. What is the one thing you're fixated on them doing better than you (their "S," your "W")? Now, what is the one thing you do better than them (your "S," their "W")? They don't even have to be in the same category. Even the playing field. You are 50 percent, they are 50 percent. Close that chapter. Then move the frick on.

Your family love is your family love. Your family is *defined* as you want to define it. Your family fun can be whatever you all love to do most, but it cannot be all the things. It can't be 100 percent. 100 percent doesn't exist. Pick your favorite 50 percent.

The thing I love most in a "mom friend" is that they're a bar-lowerer. I'm not interested in anyone who sends Pinterest pictures for the school snack or doesn't share their parenting flaws regularly. You ship my kid home from a birthday party with a plastic cup filled with crappy candy and an unsharpened pencil, I'm secretly rolling my eyes at you. If I'm honest, I can't even stand the first day of school boards and posters displaying a kid's name, age, grade, and whatever else. I'm sorry, you probably hate me now. It's just who I am, though. I loathe seeing people go through the motions, landing the wheel at "normal" when "normal" isn't something they (or others) actually *want* to do.

Ding! One day, a mom-group-text centered around my son and his friends started lighting up. It was a few days before the boys' first school dance. One of the moms started the thread, mentioning what her son planned to wear. She told the group he wanted to wear shorts, but she told him he had to wear khaki pants.

Ding! Another mom chimed in that she had the same discussion.

Ding! Another mom shared that her son was going to wear a short-sleeved dress shirt with his khakis.

Ding! Another mom thanked the group for the info and leverage to be sure her son dressed "appropriately."

Ding! I responded, "Mick didn't say yet what he plans to wear."

Here's the thing: I understand your natural tendency to want to steer your child toward looking good so you don't feel like they're going to their first dance "incorrectly." But at some point, they also need to learn that "incorrect" can be a superpower. At some point, you gotta relinquish some control, pick your battles, and not be worried about what other parents will think of *you* when your child does something different.

There is no "u" in parenting.

Later that day, Mick came home and told me he planned to wear a dressy shirt with his pajama bottoms. He wanted to 50% Rule his outfit. I said, "Sounds good."

(He didn't end up wearing that snazzy combo, but he learned it was okay to do that if he wanted to.)

You don't have to let your kids go completely rogue. Give them 50 percent leeway. Then, watch them 100 percent grow.

SECTION 6:

· · · · · · · · · · · · · · · ·

KEEP 50%ING

27
History Has its Eyes on You

We were mid-flight on our way to Greece when I saw it. I was scrolling through the movie selections when I stopped . . . oh my God! *Weird: The Al Yankovic Story* was on the screen. You may remember his story of 50% Rule musical domination from Chapter 6.

I got about five minutes into the documentary when I thought, *Hmmm, I knew a salesperson came to his parents' door to sell them an accordion, but I had no idea his father was such an a-hole.* The documentary showed a scene where his father accosted the salesman. I jotted it down in case I wanted to add it to the book.

Then, a little bit further into the film, I was struck by how many famous people were involved with Dr. Demento. There was a scene where Al was at a pool party thrown by Dr. Demento, and there was a seemingly never-ending number of celebrities showing up. Everyone from Burt Reynolds to Pee-wee Herman to Elton John was at the party. I was shocked. In the research I'd done, it was clear that Dr. Demento had a significant influence on

Weird Al. But who knew Weird Al met so many others through his association with Dr. Demento?! I jotted it down.

The documentary continued to highlight head-scratching things. I started to question everything I thought I knew about Al. How had I missed so many details? And just when I thought it was weird, it got weirder.

The movie moved on to scenes of Weird Al's struggle with alcoholism and the major fallout this caused between him and his band. And then, in walks Madonna as his love interest. Weird Al and Madonna dated?! I know I have a horrible memory, but I couldn't recall them dating. *Gosh*, I thought, *His story is more complex than I thought.*

And then, there was a scene that blew my mind and woke me up. Madonna gets kidnapped by Pablo Escobar, a Colombian kingpin and supposedly huge Weird Al fan. He uses Madonna as ransom to get Weird Al to come sing at his fortieth birthday party. The scene ends with Weird Al coming to save her, refusing to perform for the kingpin, and eventually killing Escobar after a dramatic gunfight.

I had been duped.

I should have seen it coming, but I didn't. Of course Weird Al wouldn't make a *normal* documentary; he would make a *parody* documentary. His fame and superpower came from 50% Ruling songs, making them absurd and ridiculous. So why wouldn't he do the same with his "documentary"?

His dad never assaulted the salesman. Al actually didn't drink, do drugs, or even swear. The celebrities at the Dr. Demento party? That was just them throwing every "weird" seventies/eighties star into a scene. And no, Weird Al and Madonna never dated. They actually only met once and interacted for less than a minute.

It was genius. It was on brand. It stood out.

Weird: The Al Yankovic Story also didn't have a movie-film budget. They reportedly spent $8 million on making the film, which is an order of magnitude of roughly eight times less than an average Hollywood film budget. Now, this might make sense. Until you contemplate the fact that the movie included a ridiculous number of A-list stars, including Daniel Radcliffe (as Weird Al), Rainn Wilson, Diedrich Bader, Jack Black, Will Forte, Patton Oswalt, Conan O'Brien, and Seth Green.

How did he pull that off? Because these people love him. Al built strong friendships with them over the years. Most importantly, they are completely enamored with the Weird Al vibe.

His 50% Ruling of music didn't make him great; it made him grand. As soon as he made the brave move to 50% Rule music, he earned a lifetime VIP box in a league of his own.

And, despite the "weird" premise and beer budget, *Weird: The Al Yankovic Story* received eight Emmy nominations!

Weird Rules.
Normal Drools.

And he didn't stop there. Weird Al never stops 50% Ruling.

Not only did Weird Al parody music and then parody his documentary, he also went on a tour in 2018 called "The Unfortunate Return of the Ridiculously Self-Indulgent, Ill-Advised Vanity Tour."

The name is hilarious, but The 50% Rule ninja move on this one is that he chose to end the tour at Carnegie Hall. You know, one of the most beautiful, prestigious, and some might argue, snooty venues in the world. A place where the walls are lined with pictures of Frank Sinatra, Judy Garland, and Tchaikovsky. Weird Al and Carnegie Hall—what a juxtaposed, joyful jolt!

But there was one celebrity in Weird Al's documentary I didn't yet mention. One celebrity who is a HUGE fan of Weird Al: Lin-Manuel Miranda.

I couldn't believe it. I had no idea of their association when I wrote Weird Al and Miranda (*Hamilton*) into the book. I thought they were completely separate pioneers of The 50% Rule. But then, deep into my research, I stumbled upon this magical 50% Rulers connection.

Like many of us raised in the eighties, Weird Al was one of Miranda's idols. He didn't just love his music. He was inspired by his uniqueness.

So, when Miranda finally had the opportunity to meet Al, it was a huge deal. Al was considering writing a musical and was meeting with various writers to collaborate. Miranda was known in the writing world, since his first show, *In the Heights*, was running on Broadway. But he wasn't yet Lin-Manuel Miranda of *Hamilton* fame. Weird Al asked if Miranda would meet with him to discuss the project.

Miranda recalled his first meeting with Weird Al in an interview with Jimmy Fallon on *The Tonight Show*. Talking about how he felt about Weird Al when he was younger, he said, "My dream was that maybe Weird Al would retire, and I could be the next one." Miranda went on to talk about how Al helped save him in one of his high school math classes. Miranda struggled with his grades, but one day the teacher gave the class a chance to improve their grades by doing a "creative" project. Miranda nailed the assignment by channeling his inner Weird Al. He wrote a song called "Before the Law of Sines," a parody of Billy Joel's "For the Longest Time."

Miranda told Fallon about the fateful day he first met Al: "It was like meeting Santa Claus . . . I was so nervous that I . . . self-destructed."

While sitting in a room at his childhood idol's house, Lin-Manuel Miranda threw away his shot. Rather than seizing the moment so he could at least *half* realize his childhood dream, he fumbled through the conversation, eventually suggesting Weird Al work with a different writer. Weird Al and Lin-Manuel Miranda's opportunity to collaborate ended there. Well, at least for *that* project.

Luckily, this story doesn't end all *Romeo and Juliet*—a mutual longing turned tragic misalignment. In a twist more like something out of *When Harry Met Sally*, Weird Al and Lin-Manuel Miranda found their way back to each other. In 2018, they collaborated to create "The Hamilton Polka," a corny, upbeat, Weird Al–sung mashup of *Hamilton* songs. Broadway turned hip-hop turned polka music. I mean, is there a more joyful, scenic route to a 50 percent rom-com than that?

50% worship can lead to wonderous "wedlock."

Lin-Manuel Miranda is now an advocate of other people 50% Ruling *Hamilton*. In 2016, when he handed the Broadway baton over to Javier Munoz and five other companies, Miranda said, "It was a joy to hand it off . . . now the joy is watching all of these people make it their own."

Just because you applied The 50% Rule and created something entirely new doesn't mean that's . . . it. You've created inspiration and momentum for others to take the baton and add creativity. Like the core principle in improv, you should continuously say, "Yes, and . . ."

Encourage others to build on your idea. Morph your ideas based on their input. Make it a group run AND a relay race. Pay it forward. History is meant to be continually written and changed. Or, put more frankly by Basketball Hall of Fame Coach Red Auerbach, "History can kiss my ass in Macy's window."

Your creation's graduation happens when you have the revelation that it's ready for a new destination. Only then will it get its standing ovation.

28

The 50% Rule Mutations

The 50% Rule that is plastered throughout this book is a mutation. It's not purebred. In fact, any innovation that comes from The 50% Rule inherently has an origin story. So, if The 50% Rule encourages you to take about half of something and then make the other half your own, doesn't it make sense that The Rule itself would mutate?

In this chapter, I'll highlight three mutations I've seen. I also encourage you to morph and mutate The Rule as well. If you do, and it rocks your world, I'd love to hear about it. Post about your mutation on LinkedIn and tag me (@Erin-Hatzikostas), or email hello@bauthenticinc.com with the subject line: 50% Rule Mutation.

Mutation #1—Get 50% Uncomfortable: In Chapter 3, I talked about how The 50% Rule was born. When it was an infant, it didn't carry the same message and connotation we've explored in this book. In fact, in Chapter 21 of my previous book, *You Do You(ish)*, I speak briefly about The 50% Rule but in a different context.

The original 50% Rule was a mantra I often used to encourage others to make bold, strategic decisions as they looked for their next role. I told people that with each career step they took, they should look for roles that make them 50 percent uncomfortable. That is, look at new roles where about 50 percent of what's needed is something you're familiar with and have done before. But, also be sure that about 50 percent of the new role will make you feel uncomfortable.

For example, if you're currently in product development, only move to another product development role if the subject matter makes you feel about 50 percent uncomfortable. If you're in a finance role, consider taking a strategy role in the same department. If you primarily have been working domestically, consider an international role.

Development demands discomfort.

You might say, "That sounds great, Erin. But how do you get hired into a job you only have 50 percent of the qualifications for?!" I would then gently smack you upside the head and respond, "The best jobs don't come through the HR sausage factory. You get these 50-percent roles by doing excellent work, fostering great relationships, and using authenticity as your secret weapon."

Mutation #2—Cut your goals by 50%: It's likely been less than twenty-four hours since you hit "like" on a post that encouraged you to create audacious goals, reach for the stars, or dream big. And look, I'm not saying those mantras are wrong. But I also learned that by going *too* big, you could be shooting yourself in the foot.

Last year, I read Jon Acuff's book *Finish*. If he was speaking to one person, and one person only, I'm pretty sure it was me. I looooove starting things but end up with Finish Fatigue on a regular basis. My best bet to bust through the fatigue? One of the many remedies that The 50% Rule provides to me.

But there was one I had never thought of. One that was highly counterintuitive. Cut your goals in half.

In *Finish*, Acuff talks about how setting our goals too big can lead to diminishing returns. He points to the "planning fallacy," pioneered by psychologists Daniel Kahneman and Amos Tversky in 1979. Basically, we tend to be overly optimistic when setting goals. And when we overestimate ourselves and fall short (or expect we might), bad things happen.

Acuff talks about an experiment that another psychologist, Robert Buehler, conducted with college students who were working on their senior theses. He asked each of them to independently estimate how long it would take them to finish their thesis. He asked for both a best-case and a worst-case scenario. On average, the students estimated it would take thirty-four days when, in the end, it took them almost twice that long.

So what? you might be thinking. *We are overconfident, but at least we're reaching for the stars. If we didn't, wouldn't we just do worse?*

Nope. Quite the opposite. The planning fallacy theory takes things a step further and shows that when we don't hit goals as expected, it makes us all sorts of discouraged and demotivated.

Focus less on goal setting and more on propelling.

Acuff demonstrated this through a few of his own examples as well. First, he told a story about a friend who was diligent at working out. He decided to step things up a notch and do an IRONMAN—a BIG-ASS goal. Although his friend worked out diligently about five days a week, he'd never run a race, only swam here and there, and only rode indoor exercise bikes. But he was determined to do the race. His rational mind had a plan. He was already going to the gym regularly, so he would just use that same time to train for this bigger goal.

Spoiler alert: He never did the IRONMAN. Bigger spoiler alert: He stopped going to the gym altogether!

Yes, his existing and generally over-achieving workout schedule disappeared. Gone! His big-ass goal was so big that when he didn't take action on it, it paralyzed him, so much so that in his pursuit of *great,* he killed what was *good* about his routine.

Acuff also talked about what happened in a thirty-day challenge group he led. He said that on day nine, he bopped in and told the group to cut their goals in half. Once the thirty days were over, he studied the impact of the cutting exercise. The group's performance increased by 63 percent over other similar goal-related challenges. In addition, 90 percent said they had an increased desire to work on their goal since it now seemed attainable.

And that, my friend, is *always* what we strive for with The 50% Rule: You doing big things AND being excited to do them.

What goal do you have for this week? What would it look like if you cut it in half? How about your workout goal? Can you break it down into more realistic goals? (Note: Mark your calendar on January 2nd to revisit this chapter.) What about your dream to start a business or change careers? What would the new goal be if you cut it in half?

Don't give up altogether. But I encourage you to find the rock in the river you can step on to help you make the leap without ending up soaked and miserable.

Acuff also suggests that if you can't cut your goal in half, you can also give yourself twice the time to achieve the same goal. For example, if you want to be promoted to VP, set a timeframe, then double it. If you're looking to grow your business to eight figures, pick a timeframe. Sit on it. Then come back and double it.

The name of the game is to continue to take the actions that lead to self-propulsion. Enact the Self-Determination Theory from Chapter 15. What autonomy, input, and unique 50% Rule ideas can you wrap around your half-size goal? Then, sit back and watch your head spin as you *keep* pursuing and achieving amazing things!

Mutation #3—YDKWYDK: When I told my husband I started writing my next book and what The 50% Rule was, he immediately said, "Yeah, kind of like: you don't know what you don't know." That was NOT what I was thinking, but I listened. He went on to tell me that if you listen *fully* to someone's advice, the current playbook, etc., you might miss something. There are always YDKWYDK things lurking out there. He should know. His job is to find YDKWYDKs for investigators and prosecuting attorneys.

But as I sat on his mutation of The 50% Rule, I realized he had a good point. There is no room for curiosity when our mind defaults to a follow-the-leader, 100 percent approach. There is no pause that gives us the space to think, wonder, and ask questions. And often, there is something we didn't know we didn't know that is very important . . . to know.

Just like what happened in Chapter 13 when I talked about my conversation with "Joe." He told me, in no uncertain terms, that I'd be miserable if I left my corporate gig for my ill-defined journey to something else. If I didn't have my coach supporting me and slowing me down, I wouldn't be here writing this book. I didn't know what I didn't know. And just a few months later, I would learn one of those big "not-knows" was the speaker/author/coach world I'm now ecstatically a part of.

Maybe this mutation is just another benefit. Or maybe it's a concept as old as time. But a coach once taught me that **communication is the response you get back**. And to honor that, and to honor my hubby, I think he might be onto something. Be sure to always make some room—maybe 50 percent—to discover the YDKWYDKs.

YDKWYDK: You don't know what you don't know

—or—

YDKWYDK: Yes dear, keep wowing [us with] your deep knowledge

29

The JIGSAW Puzzle

Phew! That was a lot. We're almost done with our Tour de 50% Rule. However, before we ride off into the sunset with our final story, I want to take one more water stop to reflect and pull together some of the key lessons from the book.

The book was organized by *how* The 50% Rule can impact your professional growth, leadership, business growth, and personal life.

First, we examined how The 50% Rule can help you grow professionally. We got all pumped up that you don't have to do things like others did before you. In fact, if you do things about 50% differently—in a way that is refreshing and focused on serving others—you'll be much more successful. If you celebrate and double down on your weird quirks and perceived weaknesses, you can turn your superflaws into your superpowers. But only go about halfway, because if you throw the baby out with the hot tub water, the "Rachels" in your life will probably be pissed.

Then, we talked about how The Rule can supercharge your leadership. I highlighted how your well-intentioned mentoring and advice *could* be effing others up . . . if you don't serve it with a side of The 50% Rule. Plus, if you share and encourage others to use The 50% Rule, you can motivate the hell out of them. The 50% Rule activates the primary motivator that fuels most of us—autonomy.

We then discussed how The 50% Rule can take you from authentic badass to breakthrough innovator. We heard stories of simple but innovative mashups that turned into groundbreaking success. We also talked about how great leaders and companies don't just 50% innovate, they 50% cut the shit. We saw how having the guts to go all-in on your 50% dream can create 100% success. And we capped it all off with another tool, The 50% Rule (I)nnovation Framework, intended to give complex teams and organizations a more methodical way to use The Rule to innovate.

Lastly, we talked about how The 50% Rule can be a game-changer for your personal life. The Rule gives you a simple, creative tool to stop Sleeprunning through life by helping you reinvent relationships, find work-life win-wins, and give you and your loved ones a way to do you(ish).

However, throughout the book, six (6) common themes to The Rule transcend time, place, and application. I'm certain The 50% Rule itself is the simplest tool you'll carry away from this book, but congregating around these six themes is another way to stay clear, inspired, and prepared to use The Rule to its greatest power.

Despite the Tour de France metaphor, remember that life is not a race. You're not running a defined course with orange traffic cones lining the *only* path you can travel. Instead, think of it more like a jigsaw puzzle. A puzzle where you're allowed to mix and match the pieces to curate your own picture.

And, just like the first step to solving any puzzle is to start with a single piece, the lessons in this book were scattered all over the proverbial table for you to see. But, piece by piece, *The 50% Rule* also came together to form The 50% Rule (JIGSAW) Puzzle Principles.

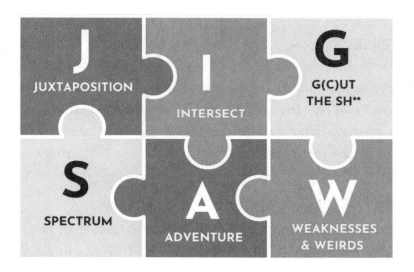

JUXTAPOSE

Juxtapositions create joyful jolts. One of my favorite principles from The 50% Rule is Juxtapose. Amazing things happen when you combine two unexpected and opposing things. We saw this when Lin-Manuel Miranda combined history about a bunch of white dudes with hip-hop music in *Hamilton*. We dove into the Pratfall Effect and how combining two juxtaposed qualities—humility and competence—can create immediate connection and trust while helping you quickly stand out in a league of your own. We also saw the beauty of juxtapositions when we talked about the relationship between Justices Ruth Bader Ginsburg and Antonin Scalia, and when my friend Christina gave us fashion advice.

Putting together two juxtaposed things, primarily because you like them and know they're not a matchy-matchy combination, is one of the coolest hacks to innovating in your life, career, and business.

INTERSECT

Earlier in the book I said the 50% Rule innovation is like setting up your two best friends on a blind date and giving them permission to make whoopee. Although mashing together two juxtaposed things often creates a "big bang," The 50% Rule is also effective when two everyday things are combined, if they've never been combined before.

For example, Merissa Beddows lit up *America's Got Talent*'s stage by combining impressions with opera singing. We learned how simple 50% Rule combinations can alter history. For example, when Whitney Houston decided to intersect her soulful soprano voice with an iconic and sacred song, she changed its tune forever. John Madden also altered the trajectory of sports broadcasting when he dared to apply his authentic personality as a coach to the traditional sports broadcasting approach.

Always remember—you don't have to forego a project, idea, or a dream because you hate the way it was done before.

Instead, you can do it your own way by creating new intersections . . . bringing in 50 percent new stuff to 50 percent old stuff. And if you do, amazing things will happen—for you *and* the millions of people who come after you.

G(C)UT THE SHIT

Cut the shit was also a theme throughout the book (or "Gut," 'cause we needed a "G" puzzle piece). The 50% Rule is simple in its definition—take half of what you like, feels like you, makes sense, etc. and then combine and curate it with your own ideas. However, sometimes you have to double down on gutting about half the shit out of things.

We talked about how Shopify did this with their meetings. They gutted their calendars so their people could focus on the work. This was a wide-scale gutting, but other times, the small cuts make a big impact. That was the case for Jen DeSantis when she made a small but bold move to walk into a meeting with a senior-level person sans fancy PowerPoint deck.

We also saw this subtly in other places. We talked about how Steve Jobs collected some powerful "dots" when he audited a calligraphy course that gave him the mastery he needed to make Apple the visually stunning brand it became. However, Jobs also MASSIVELY cut the shit when he decided to drop out of college. What he was doing and learning in school didn't align with what he needed to accomplish his goals. So, he cut it. We also saw how important it was to give others permission to cut the shit out of the advice we give them; what's a map for one person can be crap to another. Remember, if you want to be a *good* leader, focus on adding value. If you want to be a *great* leader, focus on cutting bullshit.

SPECTRUM

The 50% Rule poops on the concept of being binary. We talked about how our natural tendency to "pick sides" can have us Sleeprunning between one thing or another, too tired and dizzy to realize that we are fully allowed to land somewhere in between. We do this with everything from our politics to our vocation to our health. I told the story of my back injury ping-pong match between my physical therapist and my chiropractor. When I finally realized I could 50% Rule my health, I took *back* my power.

We do this ping-pong match more than we realize. We also see evidence of bad binary selection when we do one-half of a SWOT analysis on ourselves, pitting our "W" box against other people's "S" box. Cori Rolland and her team almost got swept up in a binary battle when her marketing overlords *initially* weren't going to allow them to deploy a unique, in-store promotional campaign. But when Cori first held tight to her side of binary, the deadlock busted, and the two "sides" found a 50% Rule compromise. You must stop picking teams and start crafting your own dreams.

ADVENTURE

If there's one thing I hope you both read and FELT from this book, it's that one of The 50% Rule's key principles is to allow yourself to go on adventures—adventures where you don't necessarily know what the destination looks like. To be honest, writing this book was one big adventure. While I had the experience of The Rule and loads of stories and notes gathered before sitting down to write it, I was amazed at what came out every time I wrote. I would often think, *Wow, I didn't realize this is where this story or chapter would go!*

Jason Sudeikis's story about how he discovered British comedy later in life, which in turn contributed to his most notable professional achievement thus far—*Ted Lasso*—is a great example of what happens when you say yes to life's little rollercoasters while slowing down enough to reflect and be inspired by them. Jesse Cole and his Savannah Bananas certainly went on many mini rollercoaster rides themselves, and the big reward came when they had the balls to go all-in on their adventure.

The rules and playbooks handed down to us should be treated less like Waze and more like Walmart greeters. They help point you in the right direction, but you shouldn't follow them home. Instead, take your own path. Run your own race. Get a little lost. Stumble through some poison ivy. Stop on a riverbank and look around for an awkward amount of time. Kick about half the traffic cones out of the way. Run, ride, walk, skip, bear crawl, and two-step through life using The 50% Rule.

WEAKNESSES & WEIRDS

Finally, the last 50% Rule Puzzle Principle is all about you getting jiggy (saw-puzzle) with your weaknesses and your weirdness.

Weird rules, normal drools. When you stop shying away from the things that make you a bit kooky and instead crank up your kookiness and shine your weird light in ways that serve others' needs and desires, that's when things get really fun . . . and really powerful.

Weird Al led the weirdo parade on this one, showing us how pumping up his weird passions created a whole new category of music and propelled him into a VIP seat on The 50% Rule bus. We also dove into how we can quickly quell the angst we harbor about our weaknesses by SWOTing them away with *our* corresponding strengths and/or the weaknesses of *others*. Yes, it is totally kosher to use snarky, petty logic to mitigate our (perceived) worser halves!

We also saw how combining a few principles of The 50% Rule can quickly make you go from underdog to unmatched. For example, Volkswagen embraced the weirdness of the Beetle and then 50% Ruled humility and competence to put their weird car on a pedestal for all to see. Ultimately, *you* can also use your Ws as the foundation to not conform to the norm, but instead, *transform* the norm!

Throughout the book, I told stories and threw out pithy quotes[4]. Hopefully, the stories and guidance made you tilt your head to the side . . . made you think about things a bit differently. Some parts probably reinforced what you already do and believe. Some things probably added a little butane to your fire. And, hopefully, you had some *a-ha* moments too.

Most importantly, just like how psychologists Edward Deci and Richard Ryan felt when conducting their Self-Determination

---

4. If you're looking for a one-stop-shop place for the quotes from the book, you can also get free quote cards by going to the50percentrule.com/quotes.

Theory experiments, I don't care how quickly you solve your puzzles; I care that you're self-propelled to keep using, encouraging, and sharing The 50% Rule. And when you do, know that I'll be cheering you on, screaming *OUI, OUI, OUI* all along the way!

30
Be the Derailleur

It's finally time to tell the story of Sam Balto, the phys ed teacher from Portland, Oregon, who went viral when he started a bike bus. Initially, I thought this was the perfect story to bring the book together and close things out with a bang. But as I started researching it, I realized I was only half-right.

For much of this book, we've talked about The 50% Rule "heroes," the people with the foresight and guts to do big things and revel in the peace, fun, and limelight The Rule brings. Their 50% Ruling won them awards, gave them fame, and made them successful. But there's one last angle to The Rule and our ride together that doesn't deserve "last place" but rather, deserves to serve as a powerful last impression.

Until now, we've talked mostly about the bike riders and the flywheels, but oftentimes, it's the *derailleurs* who quietly help others win the race.

If you've never heard of a bike derailleur, I'm not surprised. The derailleur is probably the least noticed component of a bike, but arguably one of the most important. The derailleur attaches to the flywheel, and while the flywheel keeps all the chains moving, the derailleur is what helps you shift gears.

Balto's bike bus idea started on Earth Day. Balto thought that a great way to encourage his students to be keen-on-green, while also promoting healthy activity, was to lead a group bike ride to school that day. He and some other volunteers gathered at a designated starting point. Several kids met them there, and they all took off toward the school. But much like a bus, they also gathered riders along the way. Kids joined in along the route, creating a growing swarm of (adorable) bees headed towards their hive. Many kids rode bikes. Others rollerbladed. Some volunteers rode solo. Others brought along their dogs in bike trailers. For some, it was about the transportation. For others, it was about the camaraderie.

The ride was so successful that Balto started to lead a similar "bike bus" every Wednesday, rain or shine. It grew and grew and still is going to this day. Balto often has well over 100 kids who join in on the "bus." (You have to see it to really believe and feel it, so if you want to check it out, I've included one of his videos on this book's website, www.the50percentrule.com.)

The bike bus is a fantastic example of The 50% Rule. It includes many of the components and gears encapsulated by The Rule. I was half-right; the story is a great capstone of our voyage together.

First, the bike bus certainly busts up binary. When most of us think about getting our kids to school, we think of them either taking the bus or someone driving them to school. One or the other. Do we want the convenience of the bus, with the trade-off of our kids learning "where babies come from" earlier than we'd like? Or are we able to drive them in, trading in things like more time for work or money spent on gas? In general, a kid walking or biking to school has been reserved for the few kids who live less than a mile from the school. Balto's bike bus busts apart binary, creating an entirely new option.

Balto's story is also a great example of using The 50% Rule to create something unexpected, a critical component of The 50% Rule. Being unexpected is a concept he knows well. Before Balto rose to bike bus fame, he led other unexpected initiatives. For example, while teaching in Boston, he noticed that drivers often ignored, and sometimes ran into, school crossing signs. Frustrated and determined to force drivers to be safer, he "drafted" someone he knew Bostonians couldn't ignore—Tom Brady. He made cardboard cutouts of Brady's face and secured them to the top of the signs. Drivers immediately took notice. And I don't know the stats, but I'm guessing there were limited car "sacks" of Tom Brady . . . I mean, the signs.

He also led another small-but-mighty, unexpected movement when he moved from Boston to Portland. Catalyzed by a motor vehicle hitting and killing a cyclist in D.C., he started something called the Red Cup Challenge. It was a simple plan that involved volunteers placing red Solo cups along bike path lines. Much like anything in this world, when things become too "expected," people begin to ignore them. Although bike paths are delineated by solid white lines, people start ignoring them over time. Balto said, "I want these cups to become planters, cement bollards—things that actually prevent people [from] swerving into bike lanes and force drivers to pay more attention." Ultimately, the intent of the red cups wasn't just to wake up drivers. It was to wake up lawmakers and decision-makers who could create more permanent barriers and solutions.

The Portland bike bus was also a great example of how you can reinvent relationships. The bike bus not only created a great connection between the children, it also brought the entire community together. To this day, you can see videos of people cheering on the "bus" as it rides through their neighborhood. It brought people together at a time when togetherness was more critical than ever.

Finally, Sam Balto's bike bus did something I talked about at the beginning of this book, something that is my favorite part of The Rule. The bike bus helped kids trade in discipline for desire. If he had given the children homework in gym class—*Ride your bike for at least thirty minutes today*—many would have lamented, procrastinated, or never had the time to get to their homework. Instead, by 50% Ruling exercise, the kids likely didn't even realize they were doing something that, for most people, takes a ton of discipline. He wrapped daily exercise in a big, hollowed-out Trojan Horse. Balto's 50% Rule initiative ignited the Self-Determination Theory on fire. No student was forced to join along. Instead, they were simply given the choice to join this unique opportunity.

And in their excitement to be part of something new and unexpected, many kids exercised more overall. Just like we saw in the puzzle experiment in Chapter 15, when humans are given autonomy and find intrinsic desire, they don't just do the required thing. They keep doing more of those things. The impact on the kids has gone well beyond the Wednesday ride. The bike bus ignited many of them to be more active every day of the week.

But here is where I was only half-right: As I peeled back the layers of this story, cheering on Sam Balto for his ingenious

50% moves, I realized that his story wasn't even the story you most needed to hear. That story is about Patrick Stephenson. But bear with me, we have to take a little ride to get there.

Obsess over origin to fuel your innovation adrenaline.

As I read more about Sam Balto's bike bus in Portland, I learned that Balto didn't "invent" the bike bus. Instead, he got inspiration from a similar concept first brought to life by a group called *Canvis en Cadena*, or Change in Chain, which is based out of Barcelona, Spain. They coined the term *bicibús* and aimed to spread this concept of part-biking, part-bus around Spain and the rest of the world.

So *they* were the actual inventors of the bike bus? Well, that's what I thought. But, as I dug deeper, I learned about the story that sparked Change in Chain. Their initiative was inspired by two teachers from El Petit Miguel school in Vic, Spain, who wanted to help a few students navigate getting to school through some of the rougher neighborhoods surrounding the school.

What a story, eh? Well, that's actually still not where it ends . . . or begins. The El Petit Miguel teachers took the inspiration for the *bicibús* from one of the other teachers there, Helena Vilardell. In 2015, Vilardell was feeling frustrated and helpless about Vic's air pollution. She heard about a global initiative called "30 Days of Biking," which encouraged people to ride their bikes every day in April and decided to replicate it to help lower emissions and improve her community.

Hmmm, so then who actually *started this 30 Days of Biking initiative?*

It turns out that 30 Days of Biking was started in 2010 by an American, Patrick Stephenson. In 2009, Patrick was a twenty-seven-year-old copywriter living in Minneapolis, MN. At the time, he spent most of his free time quietly tucked away, playing video games. But deep down, he harbored a childhood love for biking. He would secretly admire others, including his friend Zach Schaap, who actively biked, including to and from work. He thought it was cool, but he never thought it was something meant for the introverted copywriter living in a city where it's not uncommon for it to snow, sleet, or just be freezing cold six months of the year.

As Patrick began to vocalize his desire to bike more, Zach encouraged him to take action. Patrick began to take baby steps, hiring a personal trainer to help him shed some pounds. As he lost weight, he became more confident. He started attending biking events and immersing himself more and more into the bike scene. As Patrick started to enter the diehard zone of biking in Minnesota—the winter—he began tweeting about it, using the hashtag #winterbiking.

Then, as spring rolled around, he needed a new hashtag. Inspired by another friend of his who had started a "30 days of yoga" project, he decided to launch #30daysofbiking into the social interweb. Without much thought or planning, both Patrick and Zach started promoting the hashtag and "challenge" to others.

It wasn't discipline that fueled them; it was desire. It was a vibrational frequency that launched a movement. It was them 50% Ruling their love of biking with their friend's concept of a monthlong yoga challenge that launched a movement that is STILL going strong over ten years later.

It was Patrick's 50% Rule spark that created 30 Days of Biking. It was 30 Days of Biking that catalyzed Helena to bike to work. It was Helena's small act that inspired the first *bicibús* in Vic, Spain. It was the nine-person *bicibús* that created the global initiative led by Change in Chain. It was Change in Chain's movement that inspired Sam Balto to create Portland's Bike Bus.

And it was just one viral TikTok that catapulted Sam Balto into the media limelight as a 50% Rule hero.

A lack of limelight doesn't mean your impact is trite.

Behind every 50% Rule hero, there is *always* a spark . . . another half. Patrick Stephenson had no idea that when he took that first step towards his dormant dream—hiring a trainer—it would lead to him creating a biking movement. And he probably still has no idea how his movement sparked a global chain reaction.

The 50% Rule does NOT start with you wanting to change the world, become famous, or lead a billion-dollar company. It starts with you taking one small step. And then another. And another. It continues with your authentic desire to be bold. It explodes when you believe your actions do more than help you; they catalyze systemic, ongoing change. If you start small. Start unsexy. Start with half. You'll help others become whole.

You can do big things. You can become the next Jesse Cole. You can create something as big and well-known as Lin-Manuel Miranda. You can sing (literally or metaphorically) as loud and powerfully as Whitney Houston.

It all starts first with you shaking up the status quo by being the derailleur. Making some noise. Getting a little uncomfortable. Absorbing weird looks. Shaking things up. And, as you begin to shift *your* gears, you'll shift the gears of others too. Once you *derail*, you'll catalyze an immeasurable chain reaction. Your 50% Rule will create a ripple effect far and wide. It will inspire things you don't even know about.

What starts as *your* ride and *your* race will soon be a bike bus and race around the world. It's time for you to get riding.

• • • • • • • • • • • • • •

Let The 50% Rule be your guide, but don't forget to enjoy the ride.

• • • • • • • • • • • • •

Scan the QR code below to collect quote cards from this book!

Discussion Guide

- Of all the information presented in *The 50% Rule*, what stayed with you the most?

- What were your impressions of the author's style? Did you find the book easy to read or a slog?

- How does the book relate to your personal or professional life, and how might you apply its ideas or insights in your own context?

- Where is a place that you already use The 50% Rule? How about a place where you think you'll start using it more after reading the book?

- What is the thing you most hate doing "normal" and how might you 50% Rule it going forward?

- Did reading the book affect your optimism for your career/business/life? If yes, how so?

- How do you think understanding the Self-Determination Theory will impact how you lead and motivate others? Or lead and motivate yourself?

- What one thing taught in this book are you most skeptical about?

- What one immediate change did you make as a result of reading *The 50% Rule*?

- What one story in the book gave you the biggest "aha" moment?

- The Pratfall Effect proved that people are more likable when they disclose a blunder (or humility moment). What's a humility moment of yours that you might also start using at work?

- Did you craft an Intriguing Intro, mashing together your humility moment and your big brag? If so, can you share?

- What was the biggest lesson you learned from the Sam Balto bike bus story?

- If you could ask the author one thing, what would it be?

- Did *The 50% Rule* remind you of any other books?

- How did the book affect you? Do you think you'll remember it in a few months or years?

- How does the book compare to other nonfiction books on similar topics that you've read?

- Share a favorite quote from the book. Why did this quote stand out?

- Who do you most want to read this book?

Resources

1. **John Madden announced his retirement at the age of forty-two:** Santos, Joel, dir. *All Madden.* Fox Sports, 2021.

2. **When Alfred was growing up, he was your classic nerd:** Mental Floss. "Weird Al Yankovic's Career History (Video)." Accessed April 3, 2024. https://www.mentalfloss.com/posts/weird-al-yankovic-career-history-video.

3. **When Alfred was in college, he started to 50% Rule music:** Gemtracks. "How Did Weird Al Get Discovered? Net Worth." Accessed April 3, 2024. https://www.gemtracks.com/resources/guides/view.php?title=how-did-weird-al-get-discovered-net-worth&id=1778.

4. **For over 175 years, the National Anthem was sung and played with largely the same tempo and beats:** Kacala, Alexandra. "How Whitney Houston's 1991 Super Bowl National Anthem Became Iconic." TODAY.com, 2021. www.today.com/popculture/whitney-houston-s-iconic-super-bowl-performance-here-s-full-t208250.

5. **Jobs credits this calligraphy class for the beauty of Apple's distinct typography:** Crowe, Douglas. "Why Steve Jobs's Passion for Calligraphy Is an Important Example for You."

Entrepreneur, 2021. https://www.entrepreneur.com/leadership/
why-steve-jobss-passion-for-calligraphy-is-an-
important/377943.

6. **Jason talked about a time when he became enthralled with British shows, old and new:** Bennett, Roger. "Men in Blazers 05/03/23 Ted Lasso Pod Special with Jason Sudeikis and Brendan Hunt." *Men in Blazers*, 2023, http://podcasts.apple.
com/us/podcast/men-in-blazers-05-03-23-ted-lasso-pod-special-
with/id908407811?i=1000611594894.

7. **Neither Deci nor Ryan bought into the conventional motivational wisdom, i.e., that money is people's biggest motivator:** Ryan, Richard M., William S. Ryan, and Stefano Di Domenico. "Beyond Reinforcement: Deci (1971) on the Effects of Rewards on Self-Determination and Intrinsic Motivation," 2019. https://selfdeterminationtheory.org/
wp-content/uploads/2019/03/2019_RyanRyanDiDomencio_
Deci1971.pdf.

8. **This experiment led to the creation of one of the three basic tenets of the Self-Determination Theory:** "Self-Determination Theory of Motivation - Center for Community Health & Prevention - University of Rochester Medical Center." University of Rochester Medical Center, 2022. https://www.
urmc.rochester.edu/community-health/patient-care/self-
determination-theory.aspx#:~:text=Self%2Ddetermination%20
theory%20suggests%20that.

9. **They found that, on average, Choice Groupers worked on the puzzles over 50 percent more than the No Choice Groupers:** Promberger, Marianne, and Theresa M. Marteau. "When Do Financial Incentives Reduce Intrinsic Motivation? Comparing Behaviors Studied in Psychological and Economic Literatures."

Health Psychology 32 (9), 2013. https://doi.org/10.1037/a0032727.

10. It was the summer of 2008, and Lin-Manuel Miranda and his then-girlfriend, now-wife, left the busy chaos of New York for a much-needed vacation in Mexico: Van Evra, Jennifer. "Hamilton: 15 Fascinating Facts about the Biggest Musical of All Time." CBC, 2019. https://www.cbc.ca/radio/q/blog/hamilton-15-fascinating-facts-about-the-biggest-musical-of-all-time-1.5341556.

11. Michelle Obama referred to it as "the best piece of art in any form I have ever seen in my life.": Mohammed, Rafi. "Hamilton's $849 Tickets Are Priced Too Low." Harvard Business Review, 2016. https://hbr.org/2016/06/hamiltons-849-tickets-are-priced-too-low.

12. Mary Hamlin wrote and brought to life a play by the same name in 1917: Viagas, Robert. "EXCLUSIVE: Compare Hamilton (2015) with Hamilton (1917): First Publication of Lin-Manuel Miranda's Lyrics." Playbill, 2015. https://playbill.com/article/exclusive-compare-hamilton-2015-with-hamilton-1917-first-publication-of-lin-manuel-mirandas-lyrics-com-343516.

13. Patrice Banks, founder of Girls Auto Clinic and the sheCANic® brand, is another exemplar of the power of juxtapositions: Banks, Patrice. "Girls Auto Clinic Owner: 'I Couldn't Find a Female Mechanic, So I Had to Learn.'" *NPR Fresh Air*, 2018. www.npr.org/2018/01/09/576747854/girls-auto-clinic-owner-i-couldnt-find-a-female-mechanic-so-i-had-to-learn.

14. This realization and resolve were the impetus behind the birth of "Banana Ball," a new version of baseball that the

THE 50% RULE

Bananas invented: Hyken, Shep. "How Jesse Cole Transformed the Savannah Bananas into a Marketing Phenomenon." Forbes, 2023. www.forbes.com/sites/shephyken/2023/05/21/how-jessie-cole-transformed-the-savannah-bananas-into-a-marketing-phenomenon/?sh=19c3e1e3183b.

15. **2022 would be their last season of playing "regular baseball" in the Coastal Plains League:** "About Us." The Savannah Bananas, Accessed 3 April 2024. thesavannahbananas.com/about_us/#:~:text=In%20 2022%2C%20the%20Bananas%20announced.

16. **As of September 2023, he's written three books outlining his frameworks, routines, and relentless focus on putting fans first and "plussing":** Cole, Jesse. *Fans First: Change the Game, Break the Rules & Create an Unforgettable Experience.* Lioncrest Publishing, 2022.

17. **He thought that people who were considered "superior" (we'll call them "competent" going forward) were more likable and thus more successful when they committed a pratfall:** "Interesting Psychological Phenomena: The Pratfall Effect – Brescia University." Brescia University, 2017. www.brescia. edu/2017/06/pratfall-effect/.

18. **Instead of pretending the car was cool or perfect, they exposed its flaws purposefully:** Koraza, Toni. "Lemon: Volkswagen Ad That Forever Changed America." MADX, 2022. https://www.madx.digital/learn/lemon-volkswagen-ad.

19. **Instead of pretending like the Beetle was sleek and sexy, Volkswagen went right at the thing consumers were probably already thinking:** "The Pratfall Effect: Turning Flaws into Favours." Premium Learnings, 2023. https://

premiumlearnings.com/
turning-flaws-into-favours-the-pratfall-effect-and-its-impact-
on-marketing-success/.

20. **Instead of hiding it or being all snoozy mea culpa-y, KFC
ran ads that rearranged "KFC" to "FCK.":** "The Pratfall Effect:
Turning Flaws into Favours."

21. **Shopify's COO, Kaz Nejatian, said an engineer
marveled that the new policy allowed them to finally work
on what they were primarily hired for: writing code all day:**
Hsu, Andrea, and Stacey Vanek Smith. "Shopify Deleted
322,000 Hours of Meetings. Should the Rest of Us Be
Jealous?" NPR, 2025. https://www.npr.
org/2023/02/15/1156804295/
shopify-delete-meetings-zoom-virtual-productivity.

22. **This initial wave of 50 percenting their meetings
resulted in Shopify deleting over 300,000 hours of
meetings from approximately 10,000 employees' calendars:**
Boyle, Matthew. "Work Shift: How Shopify Culled
320,000 Hours of Meetings." Bloomberg, 2023. https://www.
bloomberg.com/news/newsletters/2023-02-14/
how-shopify-cut-320-000-hours-of-unnecessary-meetings.

23. **They should have hated each other:** Bader Ginsburg, Ruth.
"Supreme Court of the United States Remarks for the Second
Circuit Judicial Conference." 2016. https://www.supremecourt.
gov/publicinfo/speeches/remarks%20for%20the%20second%20
circuit%20judicial%20conference%20may%2025%202016.pdf.

24. **Despite being on opposite sides of the aisle on these opinions
and many others, U.S. Supreme Court Justices Ruth Bader
Ginsburg (RBG) and Antonin Scalia were the best of friends:** Cox,

Chelsey. "Fact Check: It's True, Ginsburg and Scalia Were Close Friends despite Ideological Differences." USA TODAY, 2020. https://www.usatoday.com/story/news/factcheck/2020/09/27/ fact-check-ruth-bader-ginsburg-antonin-scalia-were-close-friends/3518592001/.

25. **In fact, Justice Ginsburg said they would even pass along suggestions on how they could make each other's opinions clearer, even when they were in opposite "courts.":** Boden, Anastasia, and Elizabeth Slattery. "What We Can Learn from Antonin Scalia and Ruth Bader Ginsburg's Friendship." Pacific Legal Foundation, 2022. https://pacificlegal.org/ antonin-scalia-and-ruth-bader-ginsburgs-friendship/.

26. **Justice Scalia once said, "I attack ideas. I don't attack people . . . ":** "How Ginsburg and Scalia Maintained Their Friendship amid Professional Differences." YouTube. *PBS NewsHour*, 2020. https://www.youtube.com/ watch?v=uPgvuT-Ysks.

27. **They also shared a love for the opera, so much so that Derrick Wang created an opera inspired by them, aptly named** *Scalia/Ginsburg*: "Antonin Scalia and Ruth Bader Ginsburg's Lasting Friendship." YouTube. *CBS Evening News*, 2016. https://www.youtube.com/watch?v=ZI3c0G8iAlo.

28. **Like many of us raised in the eighties, Weird Al was one of Miranda's idols:** Travis, Emlyn. "Lin-Manuel Miranda says he talked Weird Al 'out of working' with him when they met: 'I really pooped the bed.' " EW.com, 2022. https://ew.com/music/ lin-manuel-miranda-talked-weird-al-yankovic-out-of-working-with-him-when-they-met/.

29. In *Finish*, Acuff talks about how setting our goals too big can lead to diminishing returns: Acuff, Jon. *Finish: Give Yourself the Gift of Done*. New York, New York: Portfolio, 2018.

30. It's finally time to tell the story of Sam Balto, the phys ed teacher from Portland, Oregon, who went viral when he started a bike bus: Johnson, Ron. "An Interview with Sam Balto the Teacher Who Started Portland's Bike Bus." Momentum Mag, 2023. https://momentummag. com/a-feature-interview-with-the-teacher-who-started-portlands-bike-bus/.

31. Their initiative was inspired by two teachers from El Petit Miguel school in Vic, Spain: Johnson, Ron. "Barcelona Bicycle School Bus Program a Hit." Momentum Mag, 2021. https:// momentummag.com/barcelona-bicycle-school-bus-program-a-hit/.

32. They coined the term *bicibús* and aimed to spread this concept of part-biking, part-bus around Spain and the rest of the world: "Episode 112: Climate Heroes-Biking in Spain." Duolingo Podcast, 2022. https://podcast.duolingo.com/ episode-112-climate-heroes-biking-in-spain.

33. It turns out that 30 Days of Biking was started in 2010 by an American, Patrick Stephenson: Walsh, Jim. "The Man Who Invented 30 Days of Biking." MinnPost, 2015. https://www. minnpost.com/news/2015/04/man-who-invented-30-days-biking/.

Acknowledgments

Seven(ish) years ago, my husband, Manny, and I kicked around the idea of me taking a mid-career "break." Our vision was that instead of me taking time off when the kids were infants, I would do things differently (go figure) and take a little breather while the kids were in their teenage-ish years, when their emotional and taxi-ing needs were high. Fast forward to about a year after discussing this plan, my husband and I were at a party, and I was telling a friend about how I had given my boss a firm retirement date that week. My husband overheard us and was like, "You did what?!"

Now, it wasn't quite that much of a botched communication plan—probably somewhere in between—but the point is that despite me leaving out a few details to my husband along the way, he has supported me 100 percent along the way. And of course, that "break" was never really going to be a true break. More like breathing room to do something totally new, including writing books. His gift of patience, and his faith that I could make something out of this new profession is something I will cherish forever.

The lessons I learned from my own leadership failures of the past taught me not be leadersh*t (thank you, Nicole Licata Grant, for that word!) and instead assemble a team early on to act as guides, collaborators, and 50% Rule crash-test dummies. It's easy to love your own ideas and not see their flaws or possible opportunities. The 50% Rulers group started meeting in early 2023, shortly after I started writing the book. The group has now been jamming together for over a year, and I could not be more grateful for their ideas, support, and most importantly, the energy and excitement they have for The 50% Rule.

Thank you to Adam Feltes, Alina Neuberger, Aimee Giangrave, Barret Katuna, Becky McIntyre, Beth Griffin, Bill McCormick, Cara Svoboda, Carlos A. Lacayo, Cori Rolland, Doug Shefsky, Elizabeth Sandler, Eileen A. Coughlin, Gina Manco, Heather Pierce, Hùng Phạm, Janice French, Janine Angel, Jean LaTorre, Jen Shoop, Jenn Rogers, Jennifer DeSantis, Julie Ann Dubek, Karen Hallinin, Kate Norman, Kerri Finley, Kyria' Phenix, Mari Dertinger, Marie Edwards, Mary-Ellen Cotnoir, Megan Herbert, Michelle Gardner, Mignona Coté, Mira Mambetalieva (Frankly Speaking), Rebecca Evans-Andrade, Sarah Glassburn, Shashi Sharma-Bhardwaj, and Vera Mira. An extra-special shoutout to Adam, Bill, Cori, Hùng, Jen D, and Mari for contributing your awesome 50% Rule stories and to Hùng and Barret for your early version reviews and edits of the book. Although stories of famous Rulers are fun to explore, it's real peeps and 50% Rule superfans like you who are most powerful!

I also want to thank Lydia Stevens, the Urano acquisitions editor who took a chance on me and this book. You looked beyond the "normal" publishing factors and believed in the concept and the book from the first day we met, and for that I'm so grateful.

Tina Westcott, gosh it really sucks trying to find a literary agent. So many inauthentic processes and correspondences. But not with you. You took the time to consult me, and you also decided to take on my representation, despite the fact that I was an author underdog. I think our journey is just getting started!

Suzy Swartz, thank you for stepping into *The 50% Rule* project like a lightning bolt, immediately adding energy and action to getting the manuscript into tip-top shape, and pulling together all the pieces needed to launch this book. I also appreciate your continual push to "cut the shit" from this manuscript. This book is most certainly an exponentially better version after your literary care and feeding! I was also blessed to work with a fantastic public relations partner (and so much more!) in James Faccinto. James, you didn't even blink when I told you my offbeat marketing ideas; I can't wait to fully execute our 50% Ruled launch plan!

I also have this secret weapon, Patti Hall. Patti was my book coach when I wrote my first book, and she stepped up at many a moment's notices to help me along this book's journey as well. Patti, thank you for inching me off the ledge when I had to put together that dreaded book proposal. As you always do, you reminded me to take my own medicine and do the book proposal (half) my own way. Your support, energy, and knowledge regarding all things books is something I am so grateful for.

Through the many ups and downs over the last five years, I feel so blessed to have found the two best "sidekicks" to help me run my business. Rachel Salgado has been my marketing manager, and my rock, for over four years now. Rachel is a Wonder Woman when it comes to our podcast editing, promotion, marketing materials, website design, and so much more. The pictures and diagrams scattered throughout this book are just a small sample of her kick-ass work. But most importantly, this girl never, ever feeds me a line of crap (yes, she's the "Rachel" in Chapter 9!) and for that, everything I do is so much better.

A few years after Rachel joined the team, we were lucky enough to find our other business half, Kate Walsh, who leads all things operations. Kate keeps us in order, runs our team meetings, manages our clients, and she *also* does not have a single bobble in her head; she isn't afraid to give her opinion, even when it goes against everyone else's. Having someone like Kate in my business and in my life is like having access to the most natural anti-anxiety medicine that exists.

I also want to give a massive shout-out to my podcast co-host, cheerleader, and friend of over twenty-five years, Nicole Licata Grant. Nicole is the most authentic friend I have, and her brilliance, bravery, and energy keep me forging ahead on the podcast (and all the things). As I always say about our podcast: You'll probably come for me, but you'll stay for Nicole!

To my parents, Dick and Pam Davis: I won the parent lotto with you both and am so glad you were among the very first to read early parts of this book. Dad, your authenticity is the ground zero of my passion on this topic. Mom, you are called "Perfect Pam" for a reason. Thank you both for your support and love. Always.

Lastly, to the two humans I grew in my belly and love more than anything, Ella and Mick. There is zero doubt in my mind that, despite you thinking I'm a complete dork, you will 50% Rule everything you do in life to much success. I love you, 100 percent.

About Me
(Yes, I Wrote This Too)

Photograph by: Marisa Balletti-Lavoiey from Sassy Mouth

Besides being the world's biggest 50% Rule crash-test dummy, I spend about half of my days running my small but mighty company, b Authentic Inc, where I'm an award-winning author, business coach-sultant, TEDx/keynote speaker, and podcast co-host. The other half of my days are spent Ubering my two children around to their activities, looking annoyed but secretly feeling blessed to have the professional breathing room to do it (and to get to write books while sitting in a hockey rink parking lot.)

In my teensy bit of spare time, I love to snuggle on the couch with my family while watching football, basketball, or any kind of "sports ball" (as my podcast co-host, Nicole, likes to call it). I also love to run, downhill ski, and eat piles of chocolate. Any chocolate.

The first half of my career was spent in Corporate America, working for Aetna. I loved my time there, and still can't believe they allowed me to run one of their subsidiary companies (#notqualified), PayFlex (rebranded now to Inspira Financial). Despite not really knowing what it took to be a big-girl executive and CEO, I was able to take that company from the doldrums to eventually becoming one of the darling companies of Aetna. In just three years, our earnings went from $17 million to $50 million and employee engagement skyrocketed. How did we do that? I used authenticity as my number-one strategic weapon.

And then I shocked a lot of people, including myself, when in the fall of 2018, I decided to retire from Aetna and walk away from a job and career that was humming. I actually wasn't miserable; I was simply yearning for a new mountain to climb. After fumbling and stumbling through another venture, I realized I was put on this earth for a reason: to eradicate the working world of its BS. (Well, maybe not all of it, but at least a healthy chunk of it.)

I love to speak to audiences and make them laugh, think, and take immediate action toward a more authentic approach to their career, business, and life. I also spend a lot of time working with business-to-business (B2B) healthcare and financial company leaders to help them cure their Sameness Syndrome and grow their revenue and culture in one fell swoop by deploying authenticity as their number-one strategic advantage. There's nothing I love more than shaking up their old way of thinking and helping them compete in a league of their own. If you're up for playing a different game with your team and business, shoot us an email (hello@bauthenticinc.com), connect on social media, or feel free to peruse all we have to offer at bauthenticinc.com

LinkedIn: @Erin-Hatzikostas

Instagram: @erinhatzikostas

Facebook: @b Authentic Inc

You Do You(ish) hurls aside the crusty, decades-old career advice you've likely heard for way too long: lean in, executive presence, network, blah, blah, blah. Instead, this book will help you see that there's a better way to have success and get great results. You succeed, you don't sell out.

NAMED BEST BUSINESS/CAREER
BOOK OF 2023 BY AMERICAN BOOK FEST

"IT'S ABOUT FRICKIN' TIME! *YOU DO YOU(ISH)* IS THE BOOK
WE'VE DESPERATELY NEEDED FOR SO LONG."
– **Shelley Paxton**, Former CMO of Harley Davidson & Author of *Soulbbatical*

YOU
DO
YOU *ish*

Unleash Your
Authentic Superpowers
To Get the Career You Deserve

ERIN HATZIKOSTAS

Available wherever books are sold or at bauthentic.com